10 $\frac{00}{-5}$

The
Teacher's
Voice:
A Sense of
Who We
Are

The Teacher's Voice: A Sense of Who We Are

Ray Raphael

Heinemann
Portsmouth, NH

Heinemann Educational Books Inc.
70 Court Street, Portsmouth, New Hampshire 03801

LONDON   EDINBURGH   MELBOURNE   AUCKLAND
HONG KONG   SINGAPORE   KUALA LUMPUR
NEW DELHI   IBADAN   NAIROBI   JOHANNESBURG
KINGSTON   PORT OF SPAIN

10   9   8   7   6   5   4   3   2   1

Library of Congress Cataloging in Publication Data

Raphael, Ray.
   The teacher's voice.

   1. Teachers—United States—Interviews. 2. Teachers—United
States—Biography. 3. Teaching—Vocational guidance—United
States. 4. Teaching satisfaction.
I. Title.
LA2311.R36   1985   371.1'0092'2   85-5471
ISBN 0-435-08221-3

Printed in the United States of America

For Allan and Helen

Contents

Introduction

The popular image of the teacher oscillates erratically between that of the dedicated public servant and that of the worker who gets off easy. Teachers are alternately glorified for their willingness to sacrifice their personal ambitions on behalf of children and envied for their partial escape from the rigors of the nine-to-five routine. Neither image does teachers much good. The effect of both is to make them more tense: they are always under pressure, either to live up to unreal expectations or to prove that they are not merely loafers. Yet both images have found strong and influential advocates in recent years, and teachers are becoming increasingly trapped in the pinch between them.

The Teacher as Saint

Typically, prospective teachers in education classes are made to believe that

The successful teacher is buoyant, considerate, cooperative, emotionally stable, ethical, expressive, forceful, intelligent, objective, resourceful, reliable, mature, vital, punctual, magnetic, enthusiastic, energetic, uses judgment, possesses a sense of humor, and has scholastic proficiency.

(Myron Brenton, What's Happened to Teacher? N.Y.: Coward-McCann, 1970, pp. 42–43.)

This ideal of the Super Teacher is on constant display, a vivid contrast to the inadequacies that mere mortals are likely to feel. And there is to be no slack. Teachers are expected to evidence these qualities without fail, every minute of every day. "Enthusiastic" and "energetic" are of particular importance, for a teacher must, above all, remain ex-

cited by his job. In the words of Leo Buscaglia, one of our country's most popular educators:

If you don't get excited *every* morning (my emphasis) about getting into that room with all those little kids with their bright eyes waiting for you to help them get to that table, then *get the hell out of education!* (his emphasis) Do something where you're not going to be coming into contact with little kids and killing them at an early age. There are other things you can do . . . but let children alone.

(Leo Buscaglia, *Living, Loving and Learning*, N.Y.: Holt, Rinehart and Winston, 1982, p. 36.)

The pressure is indeed intense. Should teachers really have to feel guilty for waking up a little slowly now and then? Is a teacher who reveals just a touch of lethargy at eight-thirty in the morning really killing children at an early age? And must he therefore "get the hell out of education"?

Again, consider the set of expectations which are laid upon teachers by Carl Rogers's school of educational psychology:

In accepting the student, the teacher experiences unconditional positive regard for the student's self-experiences. The teacher does not approve or disapprove of feelings. There are no reservations, conditions, evaluations, and judgments of the student's feelings but, rather, a total positive regard for the student as a person of value. The student is valued regardless of the negative feelings he expresses, feelings such as anger, envy, self-depreciation. He is accepted without condition as much when he experiences negative feelings as when he experiences positive feelings. True acceptance is unaffected by any peculiarities of the student. It is not acceptance up to this or that point and no further. It does not depend upon the student's acting or talking a certain way, upon his socioeconomic background, upon his religion, or upon his I.Q. It is not dependent upon the student's meeting certain moral or ethical criteria. It is complete and unconditional. It is a necessary element for effective teaching.

(Angelo V. Boy, and Gerald J. Pine, *Expanding the Self: Personal Growth for Teachers*, Dubuque, Iowa: Wm. C. Brown Co., 1971, pp. 10–11.)

Sure, teachers should try to accept the students and respect their feelings—but can their acceptance and respect be ab-

solutely unconditional in all situations? Realistically, how many teachers can remain so detached one hundred percent of the time? How can they possibly expect their own feelings, their own personal needs, to remain totally outside the classroom?

In the long run, the constant repetition of these lofty inspirational messages can have a negative impact upon the quality of teaching in our schools. Teachers who internalize these unrealistic expectations are being set up for disappointment. They start making demands upon themselves which they cannot possibly achieve. Unsuccessful, they become frustrated—and they tend to blame themselves for failing to attain impossible goals. The gap between the real and the ideal opens the door for nagging self-doubt: "Why isn't everything going the way it should? Where have I gone wrong?" Lacking a sense of professional accomplishment, teachers start to lose their enthusiasm for teaching—and with less enthusiasm, they experience fewer successful moments in the classroom. This, in turn, lowers their self-esteem still further, which of course leads to additional failures on-the-job. It's a vicious circle.

Alone in their separate classrooms, isolated from other adults who could give them constructive feedback and encouragement, teachers find it difficult to see that their daily frustrations and inadequacies are perfectly normal. All too easily they become like the adolescent girl who, in the privacy of her room, compares the image of the body she sees in the mirror with a model from Mademoiselle: naturally, her self-image falls short of the ideal. If she believes in the Mademoiselle image, and if teachers believe in the myth of the Super Teacher, the girl—and the teachers—will be left with a hollow feeling inside, a sense of personal failure. What the adolescent girl needs to realize is that most of her girlfriends are in a similar plight: they are real people, not magazine fantasies. What teachers need to realize is that they are not alone in the problems they face, and that it is not necessarily a sin to fall short of sainthood.

The Teacher as Economic Producer

The economic model of education places a different, but equally troublesome, set of expectations upon the teachers. According to A Nation at Risk, the now-famous report put out by the National Commission on Excellence in Education, teachers are to be seen as "the tools at hand," one of the *"essential raw materials"* of education. (A Nation at Risk: *The Imperative for Educational Reform, Washington, D.C.: The National Commission on Excellence in Education, U.S. Department of Education, 1983, p. 15)* These tools, the report claims, are not being properly utilized. *The schools are not being run at peak efficiency, and the product, as evidenced by a decline in student test scores, is therefore below acceptable standards. Part of this slack in production, the report suggests, can be made up by operating the plant more often: longer days in school and shorter vacations for the workers. But the schools must also buy better tools: that is to say, teachers. This can be done in two ways. First, the "raw materials" from the teacher credential programs must be improved; second, the existing teachers must be enticed into more efficient production through financial incentives. Competition amongst teachers is to be encouraged, for competition inspires greater effort. By following the competitive example set by private industry, our schools should be able to increase the output of quality education.*

A Nation at Risk *extends its economic line of thought to a wider setting:*

Our Nation is at risk. Our once unchallenged preeminence in commerce, industry, science, and technological innovation is being overtaken by competitors throughout the world. . . .

The world is indeed one global village. We live among determined, well-educated, and strongly motivated competitors. We compete with them for international standing and markets, not only with products but also with the ideas of our laboratories and neighborhood workshops. . . .

The risk is not only that the Japanese make automobiles more efficiently than Americans and have government subsidies for development and export. It is not just that the South Koreans recently built the world's most efficient steel mill, or that American machine tools, once the pride of the world, are being displaced by German products. It is also that these developments signify a redistribution of trained capability throughout the globe. Knowledge, learning, information, and skilled intelligence are the new raw materials of international commerce and are today spreading throughout the world as vigorously as miracle drugs, synthetic fertilizers, and blue jeans did earlier. *If only to keep and improve on the slim competitive edge we still retain in world markets, we must* dedicate ourselves to the reform of our educational system. . . .

(pp. 5–7, emphasis added)

From a preoccupation with this kind of economic competition at the international level, it is only a stone's throw to outright military jingoism:

If an unfriendly foreign power had attempted to impose on America the mediocre educational performance that exists today, we might well have viewed it as an act of war. As it stands, we have allowed this to happen to ourselves. We have even squandered the gains in student achievement made in the wake of the Sputnik challenge. Moreover, we have dismantled essential support systems which helped make those gains possible. We have, in effect, been committing an act of unthinking, unilateral educational disarmament.

(p.5)

With words like these, the National Commission on Excellence in Education proposes to turn teachers not only into productive factory workers but also into military drill sergeants, upholding our national honor as they teach the ABC's.

Of course we might attribute this aggressive, jingoistic outpouring to the expediencies of politics: it worked during Sputnik, it got money for the schools in the fifties, so why not try it again? If education can be translated into nationalism, the public will be willing to foot the bill. Maybe that's the way it has to be, but we pay a price for this type of politics. There is much to be lost by treating our schools as weapons, and one of the major costs, I suspect, is that the public becomes blinded to the creative art of teaching and to the real needs of the teachers.

I question both the wisdom and the applicability of this one-dimensional image of education. Students are not products that can be turned out on the assembly line—and neither are teachers. We do not get good teachers by processing talented people through teacher-training programs, putting them in schools that won't topple over in an earthquake, paying them living wages—and then assuming they will perform according to factory specifications. There is more to it than that. A good teacher is not produced once and then forgotten: a good teacher is re-created day-by-day.

The problem with the image of teacher-as-factory-worker is that it is based on a static, mechanistic model. So too, for that matter, is the image of teacher-as-saint. In each case the teacher is seen as a fixed, predetermined entity: a machine that produces or a machine that gives. There is no attention paid to the dynamic interaction between the teacher, as a feeling and fallible human being, and the institutional setting in which he works. The daily tensions which wear teachers down—overcrowded classes, administrative pressures, pent-up students—are systematically ignored. Nor is there any attention given to the passage of time, to the developmental processes of adulthood which teachers, as well as the rest of us, must inevitably confront.

Being a teacher myself, I would like to help rectify these superficial and simplistic images. I offer this book as an explanation of who we really are, a collective self-portrait of our workaday souls. By presenting the firsthand stories of practicing teachers, I propose to elucidate the common occupational hazards of the educational profession. I intend these personal accounts both for the benefit of other teachers, who will certainly respond to the trials and tribulations of their peers, and for the illumination of those who ought to know more about us: administrators and politicians who regulate our jobs, taxpayers who sign (or don't sign) our paychecks, and parents who don't quite understand those "other adults" in the lives of their children.

My basic message is that teachers are real people, not productive machines or saints. How strange that such an obvious message requires proof—but apparently it does, for the personal feelings, motivations, frustrations, needs, and desires of teachers are poorly understood by the institutions which employ them and by the general public. And this lack of understanding unfortunately gets reflected in ill-fated policies and reforms.

The easiest way to understand people is to meet them. That's what this book is all about. I have sought out scores of teachers—good teachers, most of them—and listened to the stories of their jobs and their lives. From these I have selected a handful of autobiographical sketches to present in these pages. The teachers talk of their ideals and their inspirations, and also of the problems they face in school. They talk, too, of how their work fits in with the overall fabric of their life situations. They speak of the conflicts between their individual needs and the educational institutions which stifle those needs. And they speak, inevitably, about their continuing search for growth and development through their work—and their never-ending struggle to stave off fatigue.

What I discover from these interviews is that a career in teaching does not adequately evolve with the passage of time. The profession seems ill-equipped to counteract the cumulative fatigue caused by common daily tensions and institutional pressures. "Teacher burn-out," as it is popularly called, is a widespread phenomenon, and its causes are deeply rooted in our institutional structures. To counteract the tendency toward burn-out, we need to develop ways in which a teacher's job can be flexibly structured to permit more professional growth and development. There is no educational reform that takes precedence over teacher rejuvenation. A stimulating classroom environment is dependent upon teachers who still believe in themselves and in their work.

In a general sense, this book is not limited to the subject of teaching; it is an exploration into the relationship between time and work, and an examination of the impact that these basic elements can have upon our personal sense of well-being. It is a story of our perpetual quest for individual meaning within institutional settings. I hope it will be an inspiration to all of us, teachers and nonteachers alike, who seek to keep the energy flowing.

Chapter One
The Teacher's Career

The self-portraits which follow are to be viewed as candid pictures, snapshots taken of specific teachers at specific points in their lives. There is no suggestion here that a teaching career progresses along linear lines, but rather that the diverse problems which teachers face are a function of time as well as circumstance.

The teachers were not randomly selected. I have tried to represent a reasonable cross-section of grade levels and work situations—big schools and small, public and private, urban and rural—but in all cases I was looking for one important criterion: self-knowledge. I chose people with a firm sense of themselves for artistic, not scientific, reasons: in telling good stories, they illustrate with personal insight and clarity the occupational hazards of the teaching profession.

These self-portraits were tape recorded, dutifully transcribed, and then edited only slightly for the sake of cogency. I have tried to retain the immediacy and the experiential authenticity of an oral tradition. Purposely, these stories lack the conscious contrivances of the written word. They are offered here as spoken representations of our real-life experiences.

Because of the personal and sensitive nature of these stories, several of the teachers you are about to meet have been given pseudonyms to protect their future careers.

student teacher, primary grades # Sarah Rosen

When I went into the credential program, I was prepared for the worst. Everyone says: "The education classes, you just have to get through them." But I had some good professors. They were really interested in me as a person, and who I was and what I was going to be doing. They took their time to get to know me, and I appreciated that. A lot of people said: "They haven't been in classrooms for years, and they'll teach you all this irrevelant stuff." I didn't find that completely true. For the math professor it was certainly true, and the social studies teacher tended to be more traditional in her approach, but in general they seemed to be up on the current trends in education and the philosophy of education.

Yet there's something kind of strange about this program. They tell you that unless you go into special ed. or bilingual education, there are no teaching jobs. They told us that the first day we were there, and they continued telling us in various ways throughout the semester. So here I am finishing in two weeks, and I say to myself: "Well, I'll just go look for a waitress job. I'll go to work in a store or something." The university is training me for something they don't believe I can get a job in. It's like: what am I doing? And why?

The schools get a pretty good deal out of student teachers. You don't get paid, and of course you're not working anywhere else because student teaching takes so much of your time. Meanwhile, you're paying tuition to the university. They get all this free labor from us. Not only is it labor, but we're the new people with the new methods and the new ideas. With one of my teachers, she was burnt-out and wanted a student teacher to come in and do the work. She was real receptive to all these ideas I had, but I said to myself: "I'm not getting paid; she's getting paid." I didn't want to put that energy into it when she was getting paid and I was just the student teacher.

It isn't only the pay—it's that it wasn't my class, and I couldn't do it exactly how I wanted. For me to go into her classroom and implement what I believe to be a good educational program, I would have to completely redo everything, including her seating arrangement. She wouldn't have let me do that. What they expect student teachers to do is to bring in all these fun activities for the kids. You have to have your educational objectives and your behavioral objectives and all that stuff, but it's supposed to be fun and it's supposed to last thirty minutes and then it's over with. It doesn't matter if you were there the day before or the day after. That isn't a realistic view of what teaching is all about. Teaching is everything from your bulletin board to getting the kids to line up.

Before I went into it, I had nightmares about student teaching. I felt like it was an ordeal that I had to get over with. I heard it was the worst time in your life; you're doing all this work, and it's real hard.

The first day I walked into the classroom, I didn't know what I was going to do. I planned to sit back and watch and then talk to the teacher after the class about what I would be doing. I went in there open, ready to learn from my master teacher. I had heard such good things about her. My supervisor had just raved about her: "She's the most incredible kindergarten teacher."

But I didn't see any of it. I was just horrified with what she was doing to some of these children. She was trying to train them, to regiment them, so they would follow her commands, all of her directions. They would stand up all together and sit down all together. There were thirty-two children. At least a third of them spoke no English. She had them all doing the same work at the same time. It was the first week of school for these children. Most of them had never even gone to nursery school.

Of course there were behavior problems. I would act badly in that situation too, not understanding what's to go on. "Why do I have to color this? What do I do now that I'm finished?" So they'd start walking around the room, which she didn't like. They'd make a little noise. "No talking!" She didn't want them to talk to their neighbors.

She was teaching them the alphabet. Every week they'd get a different letter. She'd hold up the letter A: "Take your red crayon. Trace around the outside of the A." Then she would have them color it in. Well, for a five-year-old who can't write or anything, to color in the lines can be very difficult. Then she'd give them checks, grade them, whether or not they colored okay. She gave them a happy face if it was okay. Some of them, she'd say, "Do over." She had these little stamps that said things on them. Some of them would say "Messy," or something like that. Five-year-olds—it might ruin their whole career.

I said to her the second day I was there: "Maybe I could sit on the rug and read them a story when they're finished with their work. They could come and sit down." She told me: "This is not a private school. We do not individualize here." I almost cried. Everything they taught us at the university about individualization, children with special needs, adapting lessons—where was it? I was just shocked.

And the thing about not talking. All the tables were set up in groups, eight children in a group, so they're facing each other. Five years old, and not to talk for three hours of the day? Well, not only is it hard for them, but why shouldn't they talk? Here's the time they should be making friends and learning communication skills or whatever, and it's not allowed. When they went out to the playground, the fifteen minutes they were out there was the only time during the day to relax and run around. And a lot of times she decided she would teach them a game instead of letting them have free play at recess. Her idea of a game was like "Duck, duck, goose." She had the children all stand on a line, and one child ran around. About eight children got a turn out of thirty-two. The others just stood there like statues for their fifteen minute recess. Then she marched them back into the classroom. That was their physical movement for the day.

Toward the end of the time I was there, and as I was gradually taking over the class, it relaxed—probably because I was doing more with them. Sometimes she let me do things that she didn't agree with just because she thought: "You'll learn from it. You have to make your own mistakes." But I never felt they were mistakes. I always thought things went pretty well.

You know, it's funny. On a whole other level, I got along with her fairly well. She had trained a lot of student teachers and was good about telling me what my responsibilities were and making it really clear what I was going to be doing. Also, she was real easy to talk to. *Too* easy. When we were having recess, she would spend all this time telling me who she had dinner with the night before rather than talking or playing with the kids. The children would be fighting or crying, and she'd ignore them.

There was one child who had severe behavior problems. I was really impressed at first that she took all this time to bring in a psychologist and a social worker and the mother and the day care worker and all these other people to discuss the problem. But it was mainly because she wanted the kid removed from the class. She felt that if she could prove the child had severe problems, she shouldn't have the child in her class. She showed me these weights. She told me, "If he really gets out of hand, I have weights for him." I said, "Oh, what a good idea," thinking we could get him to work out with the weights a little bit, burn his energy off. No. These were weights to hold him down to the chair. They put weights on his wrists so it's harder for him to move, to walk around the classroom. This poor little five-year-old could hardly move with them on.

Another interesting thing that happened: she was doing a "Me" unit, and she had them color a picture of a person. All the girls had to color a picture of a girl with a skirt and very Caucasian features, and all the boys had to do a boy figure. She showed them how to do it: "Color the hair like this, then color the shirt and color the pants." She, of course, colored the hair blonde, the shirt red and the skirt blue. At least three-quarters of the class colored it exactly like she did. This was supposed to be "Me." The majority of the children in the class were not white. There were a lot of Chinese, Vietnamese refugees, and some blacks—and on their pictures of "me," they all wound up with blonde hair.

The first week we were there, she had all the non-English speaking children sitting at one table, all the children who she felt came from higher families or were a little smarter at another table, and then two tables with a mixture—she didn't know quite where to place them. I said to her, "Don't you think it would help the non-English speaking ones to sit with the other ones?" She said, "It's too hard when we start grouping them for activities to have them mixed." Well, for the seven weeks I was there, she never did one activity where we had them in groups, so it didn't seem to matter. They all did the same thing anyway.

She didn't bother to communicate with the non-English speaking kids. She ignored them completely. I would say to her, "I don't think so-and-so got the activity." She'd say, "That's too bad." Most of the ones that didn't speak English were fairly bright anyway, and as soon as they learn the language they'll speed right ahead. So I wasn't that worried about how they were doing academically. I was more worried about how the kids were doing emotionally in this program— what their image of school was turning into. It wasn't very fun. It was pretty boring. They did a lot of coloring dittos.

That's all they did was dittos: ditto this, ditto that. The teacher just told them: "This is what you're going to learn. Here's the ditto. Now learn it." There was no education where they were responsible for what they learned. There was no discovery, no exploration or observation work. Those are the kinds of skills that supposedly we should be teaching at that age.

My other student teaching experience, the second-grade class I'm working in now, is totally the opposite. It's very child-oriented. The teacher is all individualized. Each child is working at their own speed. We have children who read at fifth-grade levels and children who don't read at all. It's all activities. The children are constantly doing art work and making puppets and putting on puppet shows. There's so much learning going on there, and the children are doing it themselves. We give them the materials, and they see what they can learn from it. That is so much the way education should be. The teacher should be there to guide the activity, but not to tell them what they're going to learn.

It's not in a public school—it's a community school. I'm not sure I can ever find the kind of situation I want in the public schools. But I am very interested in education and I like working with children. I want to be involved in the educational process. One thing I'd like is to have my own nursery school, because that way, I'd be doing the kind of education I want—and I'm also the boss. That appeals to me.

When I think about teaching in a public school, it seems very isolated to be in a classroom alone. Student teaching is different, because you're with another teacher. You're constantly talking and discussing the children and discussing what you're going to be doing. You have feedback. Someone else's ideas are there. You have two people. It's team teaching, and it's a completely different thing. If I taught in a classroom, I'd look for a situation that was team-taught.

I think part of the reason that teachers stagnate, like this kindergarten teacher that I had, is because she's isolated in this room, and she's not seeing other teachers work. She's not up on the newest teaching things. I went to a seminar a couple of weeks ago where this guy did research and proved that a majority of teachers, even if they take a class on new methods in education, rarely adapt it to their teaching practices—unless there is another teacher in the room, and they're doing it together, and there's feedback and support and all that.

I guess a lot of people like the isolation, because they can close the door. It's a freedom, in a way. There's no one looking over them and no one competing with them and no one criticizing them. It's also a lot of power. It's scary when you think of these teachers—they're almost like dictators. They have these thirty children under their command; they can do anything they want with them. I don't think it should be that way. That's not education. If I was a child with a dictator teacher like that, I would not learn anything.

I have very high standards of education, and I don't know if I'll ever see them in practice. My supervisor said to me: "I hope you don't have any more criticisms." He's so sick of hearing me criticize these teachers. But I do have criticisms, even of my present teacher. Her class is pretty good, but she's human and she has faults and she's lazy sometimes. Personally, I think she's doing a half-assed job most of the time. I'm not sure why: is she tired of teaching, too? She's only ten years older than I am, but sometimes she comes in in the morning and she'll say, "I'm so tired today, I don't feel like doing anything. We'll just let them color." She's letting her personal life affect her teaching, which I don't believe in. I've gone to work tired too, but it's not the kids' fault.

I often wonder why people would continue teaching if it's such an awful experience. Lots of people feel it's a lot of hard work and there are no rewards. There are so many teachers out there who are hurting children by just going to work every day without being enthusiastic and without loving it, and I don't even know if they like children anymore.

It's just like a doctor performing an operation: if he no longer knows how to do it, I wouldn't want him performing on me. Just because he has his medical degree and everything, why should he continue practicing if he's not curing people? Why should a teacher continue teaching if the children aren't learning? Maybe there should be a little farm where old teachers can go. . . .

Maybe these older teachers, when they started out, had high expectations. Now they're burnt-out. They might be disappointed in that teaching hasn't been all that they thought it was going to be. Partly it comes from them, too: if they had been a different sort of person, perhaps they would have found what they wanted.

It depresses me to think about it. It almost makes me not want to go into teaching. I don't know if it's the system that does it or if it's the kind of person they are. If it's the system, it seems to me that it's discouraging teachers very effectively. I hope it's just the type of person that they are, because I don't think I'm that type of person. I hope that after twenty years of teaching, I will still have the enthusiasm that I have now.

Actually, I cannot envision myself doing one thing for the next twenty years, doing the same type of work. I don't think I will get tired of it, because I'm the type of person who will immediately, as soon as it's dissatisfying, start looking for something else. I need that constant challenge of a new experience.

But again, there are so few teaching jobs that you feel if you have one, you'd better not give it up. Like this one teacher I had, she has so much sick leave added up, she could actually take a couple of years off. I asked her, "Why don't you do it?" After you take a sabbatical, you're not guaranteed the same grade, the same class. She likes where she is, so she's stuck until she retires in another twenty years.

The teachers in the public schools, there's so much concern about the *job*: what your union is doing, how much you're getting paid, if you're getting paid for what you're doing. I feel, and I know a lot of other people feel, that teaching is not just a job. It's more of a profession, where you're putting your whole self into it and you're doing a lot of work that you're not going to get paid for. If you want to be a good teacher, you have to be willing to do that.

In a way I don't feel justified criticizing older teachers because I have not done it myself. Maybe if I had taught for twenty years, or even five or ten years under these circumstances, I would feel like they do: I'd say, "It's not worth putting all my effort into it, because the rewards are so small." But I'm not in their shoes, and I don't plan to get caught there. Seeing them, I'm analyzing what situation they're in and I'm deciding I don't want it. I won't let it happen to me.

I would take a teaching job at the moment even if it wasn't the ideal one, just to get some more experience teaching in different situations. I can't afford to just keep looking till I find the ideal situation. And I'm also sort of curious to see how much of a bad situation I can take and what I can do with it—you know, how I can change it.

Lynda Kime

first-year teacher, fourth grade

I'm not sure whether you can ever be ready to be a teacher from just going to college. This year, for me, has been totally different—even though I've had quite a bit of experience as an aide and a student teacher. Having the class to yourself, and not having somebody else you can depend on in case you fail—you can't even imagine what that's going to be like until you're actually doing it. You can only be prepared up to a certain point, and the rest of it is just throwing you out there and letting you do it.

I love the feeling of control—to have my own classroom. I had a real hard time being an aide last year. I just wanted to be in there by myself. I wanted to be able to do things my way—if I wanted to teach language in the morning and then do reading, just to be able to do that. And to have the freedom to try new things in my own classroom, which you don't have as an aide and you don't have as a student teacher. I would have gone anywhere to teach this year. I didn't spend six years in college just to be a substitute. I wanted to be in a classroom every day, and to set things up the way I wanted to set them up.

I don't remember ever saying to myself, "Now I want to be a teacher." It was just something that I always wanted to do. I wanted to work with children in some capacity, and that seemed to be the best way to be able to do it in a situation that was somewhat structured—not just a recreation director for the summers. I've grown up with the idea of being a teacher. If somebody would have asked me when I was a kid what I wanted to be when I grew up, I'd have said a teacher. Actually, I even did some teaching when I was a kid. I started working in a school when I was in eighth grade, just going over and volunteering, because there was an elementary school by my junior high. I'd walk over there and spend an hour, two days a week.

I never wanted to be anything else, not as a career. I spent some time working as a manager of a store, in conjunction with working as a teacher's aide, and discovered first of all that you deal with the same kinds of problems with adults as you do with children. So when I hear people say, "How can you deal with children every day?"—it's not really different. When I was a manager, the people who worked for me were sometimes more difficult to deal with as adults than most of my kids in my class.

Plus teaching is never boring. It's different from day to day, regardless of whether you are doing the exact same thing. Kids' reactions to each other, to me, to what they're doing, are always changing. For me, that's really exciting. It keeps my energy level up. I like the constant change, and the fact that it never gets routine.

I'm definitely inspired. I love what I'm doing. Coming to work in the mornings is like . . . well, I really enjoy being here, teaching and being with the kids and interacting with them. They're genuine, most of them. They get to a certain age where that kind of changes, but I don't think it changes too much in elementary school. You can give a lot, and it seems like just when you get to the point where you've given all you can give, one of them, or ten of them, or all of them, seem to sense that and they put back into you. That charges you up so you can go and go and go until you get to that same point—then somebody else, and it's always a different kid, will put back into you again.

There are different personalities in kids which meet almost every need an individual could have. There are kids in here that are bright, and they meet one need; there are the kids that are slow that meet a whole other need. Those are the kids that really need you to be there to help them, to encourage them. That makes you feel good, even important. The ones that are bright could probably go right straight through and not need a lot of assistance, and yet they give you something else. You get all this feeding into one individual in one classroom and it's like . . . I don't know why it's not something that everybody wants to do.

I work hard. I get here at seven-thirty. School starts at quarter-to-nine. I really like that. That's my freshest time. I can get a lot done in that hour before the kids get here. Then at eight-thirty the buses arrive, and that's one of my favorite times of the day. We're not in an academic situation yet, and yet the kids come in and they can tell me, "Last night we did this." It's my time to feed into what's going on with them on a personal level. I'm always in the room at that time. If I have dittoing, or things I need to talk about with other teachers or the principal or whatever, I try to do it before eight-thirty, so that I can spend that last fifteen minutes in here with the kids who want to come in early.

When the kids go home at two-thirty, I don't get anything done because most of the kids that live in town come right back. They feel good about what goes on in this room and they know it's okay for them to come in here after school. I usually stay here till around four o'clock. I get home at about four-thirty and give myself a couple of hours to relax and eat dinner. Then I usually start up again at about six or six-thirty and go till nine or nine-thirty. Not every night, but a good three or four days a week, depending on how much I have to do and how much there is to correct. That's the worst area, correcting. It just takes so long. I don't want to sit and correct papers; I want to start working on something coming up that I'm really excited about.

Weekends, I spend probably two or three hours on Saturday and about four or five on Sundays. I try to leave Saturdays as a day for me, but it doesn't always work that way. About every fourth Saturday I go to the Teachers' Center in Eureka, because they have a lot of good materials. That's an all-day shot. But Sundays are my day for school. I spend from about noon or one o'clock to maybe five or six. Or if I'm doing something during the day, I'll use Sunday evenings for my school time.

I don't have a whole lot of time just for myself, for the "nonteacher me." I'm dating somebody, so I try to spend time with him. Fortunately, he's also in education. That's really nice, because I can share my feelings about my class and what we're doing. I can feed off of him and say, "What do you think of this idea or that idea?" We have the ability to give each other constructive criticism and say, "I don't think that's going to work." I couldn't be dating somebody this year who didn't share my interest in education, because it would be too conflicting. I'm just too keyed into what I'm doing. I talk about it all the time, because that's the whole focus of my life. I'd drive somebody who wasn't interested in education nuts. A lot of my friends from college—I really don't see much of them anymore, because my life is so centered. I can't just pick up and go out in the evenings, because my responsibilities are so different now. I've probably changed more this year than I ever have, as far as a social life is concerned.

Usually on Thursday night I'll make up a batch of cookies, because on Fridays I like to have a treat for the kids. It's not a reward/punishment kind of thing. You don't get a treat because you've been good or you don't lose it because you've been bad. It's a thing for us just to share time together. That's what makes it special, and that's why I do it. I enjoy cooking for them, because I know they enjoy it too. It's not a thing they take for granted. They always say thank you. I don't ever tell them in the morning what I brought. It's like a big game we play all day. They try to trick me into telling them what I brought for their treat.

I don't make a big issue of the fact that we do treats in our class. I don't want it to be a thing where other teachers feel that they have to do it too. And the kids don't make a big deal of it, either. They don't run around to the other classes and say, "We get a treat every Friday!"

I try to get along with the other teachers, but it's more difficult for me to deal with teachers sometimes than it is to deal with students. I can spend more time trying to figure out how a teacher feels about something I've done or said, or about me, than I ever do with a student. As a first-year teacher, it can be real hard to have any kind of credibility. That is the area that frustrates me the most. Granted, there are things I don't know about, but I'm real open to that. I will be the first one to say, "Boy, I blew that one." But at the same time, I feel like I have a lot of common sense about dealing with kids. When that's challenged in me just because I'm a first-year teacher, it irritates me—especially coming from a teacher that doesn't really relate to their kids. Those are usually the ones who are most critical of first-year teachers or student teachers. Unfortunately, they usually seem to be a strong teacher on the staff, somebody who people try to get to approve of what they're doing.

I don't feel that there's always a lot of support as teachers for one another. Sometimes it's just: "You do your thing in your room, and I'll do my thing in my room. Don't observe me and I don't want to observe you."

It gets to the point where it's competitive: "You're not going to get any of my ideas, and I don't want any of yours, because everybody is going to be comparing us."

That's not at all where I'm at. I work a lot with the third-grade teacher. We do a lot of things together; we share a zillion ideas; we're going to a four-day workshop together. We're about the same age, we commute together, we have the third and fourth grades, plus the fact that we're both real open to sharing ideas. I think the more time teachers spend together and share ideas, the better everybody is going to be.

It's been real neat for me to go to a couple of conferences

since I started teaching, even if it's a weekend. I don't mind taking my Saturdays or Friday nights. It's so much different to hear someone say, "This is a good idea," or "Try this game," when you have your own class and can try it out with particular groups and particular levels. No matter how much time you spend in college . . . I wish now that I would go back and take some of my Ed. courses again, because I could apply them right now, and I know I'd listen better. I'd be more aware: "Oh, I could use this. I could use that." That's the thing about getting ideas from other teachers that's so neat: if you get the idea right now, you can apply it to a specific situation in your class, and not two years down the road when you get a job.

To me, that's what teaching is: learning from other teachers. If you don't learn from other teachers, then you get stagnant—and once you're stagnant, you might as well hang it up. If I got stagnant next year, I have enough background in other things that I would leave it, because I don't want to be a mediocre teacher. If I can't be a good one, I'm not going to be one at all. I feel more strongly about that than anything, because there are too many mediocre teachers. Some of them get to the point where they think: "There's nothing else I can do; I only have a few more years to put in." So they just stay with it, for whatever reason.

I can see how people get burned out, because you give so much all the time. And it takes so much time. I can't imagine coming in and dealing with kids and working on curriculum and correcting papers and doing all that if you're not really interested in it anymore. It's just too much work. I can see where you'd get to the point where you'd go: "Ahhh, I just need a break!" But I also know teachers who have never gone through that—they were just gung ho until they were sixty-five and retired. My aunt was a perfect example of that. She taught sixth grade for twenty-five years and just loved it. Every year was like a whole new world and a new challenge. But that was the only thing in her life. She was a widow, and had been for a long time. Her whole focus was on her teaching.

For me, I can't see looking at teaching as just another job. But I don't really think of it as a career, either. Somebody who thinks of their job as a career is somebody who's always looking for something above what they're doing, a promotion. I don't feel that way. I have no desire to be a principal, which is the next step up. I mean none. At this point, I don't even have any desire to have my master's. I realize I'd make more money, but I don't really need a master's because I don't intend to teach college. This is the age level I like. I like teaching elementary school.

To see the kids growing, that's all I need. If I see a kid take a step in the right direction, that makes it all worthwhile. You may beat your head against a brick wall for months, and then they move forward a little and it's like "Yea!" I get as much from the kids in the room as I give them. It's always a two-way street. That's exciting. It's nice to put in and put in and put in—and then see them grow.

Rae Johnson

fifth year, third through sixth grade

Initially, when I first decided I wanted to teach, I had the idea that school socializes kids, and that someone who has a good idea about how human beings should interact could provide experiences for kids at a real basic level that would help . . . well, that would help the outcome. That was my philosophy: you give these young human beings an opportunity to respect each other, to respect their materials and the people they're working with, and that out of it would grow people with more sensibility. I wanted to work with these kids to give them a certain kind of emotional background—as well as the skills. The skills were important, but I was more interested in the socialization process. I wanted the kids to be true to themselves, and to be sensitive individuals who could care about each other and love each other and love their world—instead of being violent and destructive.

Over time, I've had to modify these ideals dramatically, to balance the needs of the students, the teacher, the parents, and the community. And the institution. Like the parents want their kids to do certain things in school, to learn certain things, and if the kids don't learn those things, then the parents come back to you and want to know what's going on. And the kid wants to learn certain things, and of course the bureaucracy, the county, also has certain things—and it's not always compatible. You end up having to balance it. You can't necessarily just cater to your one ideal. You can't just do all the group processes and group projects that you want, because there are individual kids with individual needs in terms of how they learn. Some kids learn well orally, other kids learn better by writing things out. Some kids need to do more math, other kids need to do more reading. So the pressures of all those different areas make it impossible to simply create an educational environment that satisfies that goal of "right living."

Somewhere, I've still got that goal—but it seems a lot further away because the day-to-day has really taken over. That's one measure of how burned-out I am: whether there's any vision going on, or whether it's just day-to-day. You know: "Oh, what am I going to do tomorrow? Let's see, I've got to get this done and that done and this done."

When I first started teaching, I'd ask: "Where are they in their learning process? What's the next step?" I'd get some idea of what I wanted to teach, and then I'd just sit around and brainstorm about it: the different ways I could present it, and who would understand what things. Now it's like: "I've got four time slots of so many minutes, and I've got to fill each one of them, and what am I going to stick in them? What haven't I covered on the contracts? How much time do I have? Which aide will be in my classroom tomorrow? Who do I have to work with?" Balancing all the exigencies of what's going on. The outwardness of it as opposed to the inwardness of it. It just makes it that much less exciting. It's a gradual wearing down, which is a real natural process.

The students' attitude, too—over time it just wears away at you. You know: "Aren't you gonna do something exciting for me? We pay you to work here, so you better teach us something. Show us your tricks." I used to laugh—literally laugh—when they fed me that stuff. It would make them mad, really angry. I'd say, "Oh, poor baby! You have to sit and do this work!" And I'd pat 'em on the head. Boy, you should've seen the fire coming out of their ears. But it didn't get to me. I could smile and say, "I'm just here to do what I'm doing, and if you want to have a snit about this you can have it. It doesn't bother me."

But now it gets under my skin. Now I think I would rather be at home sitting in front of the fire reading a book. Let's not bother with this. I don't have to be here for this kid.

When I get worn down like this, I'm more likely to lose control. There's only one time I got outrageous in the classroom and did something that later I wished I hadn't done. All year long there was this thing about the chairs. They weren't all the same—it was just whatever we could find from wherever they came from. You'd think that they'd just be glad that there were any chairs at all, 'cause when we first moved into this place we didn't even have any chairs. But no, they had to fight about the chairs. It was a constant hassle. I tried and tried to let them know that it really bothered me, and that as far as I was concerned one chair was as good as another. But every day I would have to ignore some hassle about the chairs: people pulling them away from each other or knocking something over trying to drag them around. So it was real near the end of the year, and I was tired and edgy. This one morning everyone came in to start school and I was trying to organize myself and I heard all this fighting behind me. I turned around and Rebecca and Charlie were in a fist fight over the chairs. I walked over and I grabbed each one of them by an arm and opened the door and *threw* them out one by one. Thunk! Thunk! You could hear them land. I walked back in and was immediately so remorseful and so upset and started to cry. I couldn't believe I had done such an off-the-wall thing. It was a classic case. Really, how can a thinking adult even care whether two kids argue over a chair? I mean, you don't even need to worry about it, but over time it drives you out of your mind. It just wears away at you, bit by bit.

Right now, I'd say I'm at a decision point: I have to decide either to take teaching more seriously—or to take it less seriously. I don't want to be just drifting around, slowly losing my drive. When you no longer have any enthusiasm for working with kids, then really what you're teaching them is that it's no fun to learn things. Because there you are: you're having a miserable time. And kids are really perceptive; they know what's going on. If you're having a bad day or you're bummed out, they can tell. They see it. And so you're communicating with your body all these feelings to them. Kids can pick up all the ideas and impressions and imprint all these things. So trying to maintain some kind of a positive attitude toward the kids makes a big difference—unless you don't care whether they have any kind of joy in what they're doing.

Of course you can't maintain a positive attitude all the time. Sometimes I wake up in the morning and I don't feel very positive at all. But I just go to school anyway and teach. If it's not real extreme, I look around and I think, "Oh, here I am again. Now I have to do this." And I just do it. I just think about what needs to get taken care of, and answer the questions that need to be answered, and stuff like that. I don't really make any strong connection with the kids. But if I'm so removed from it that I'm not there at all, then I can get impatient because they're not understanding things, but I'm not there to explain them. I mean, even when I'm explaining them, I'm not there. I'm not monitoring the feedback. Or there can be discipline problems, because my weird energy creates other weird energy around me, and they all get weird too. Or it can turn into a sort of lackluster situation where nobody really likes what they're doing, but they're just doing it.

And then sometimes I can go in when I don't have much energy and they can be in this great mood and totally change my head around. They can provide the energy; they can get me up. Some question or thing that they do will make me feel better, or we'll have a great conversation or discussion or something like that. Then I really appreciate it. I remember why I like working with kids, which is that they're real "at the moment," and they don't let themselves get bogged down— as much—in all the other things that are going on in their lives.

Kids can take you all the way up or all the way down. Sometimes they make me feel like a nag. "Close the door. Close the door. Please close it. Please close the door." It gets me so frustrated. Why can I not get across to these kids the simple, basic things of how we all get along together? I mean, how many group discussions and group processings do we have to have before they'll stop smashing each other in the face? It makes me feel real inadequate, because I feel like I put a lot of energy into that part of the school scene. Sometimes it just makes me say, "Screw it. I don't care about teaching these little kids anything. If they can't have enough respect to at least put their fifty percent into the situation, then *I* don't care about *them*." It just makes me feel *bad*.

When I have bad days like that, I get real introspective. I start taking myself apart. You know, self-doubts and guilt— and lack of clarity. I reflect on all the things in my life that are making it hard for me to be a teacher, and I berate myself about that. And then it spills over into all the other stuff that isn't done, like the ordering and the people I was supposed to talk to and the things I was supposed to sign.

I start to think that I could be doing *everything* better. I get down on myself because I'm not doing the job I could be doing. I have really high standards for myself. And that's one thing I have to come to terms with in working with kids: it's not necessarily fair for me to have the same standards for them as I have for me, because the standards I set for myself are ridiculously high.

I have to constantly remind myself that these are fourth, fifth, and sixth graders who can't possibly match up to my standards. But the more I check in with their humanness and talk with them about what they *are* learning and what they want to learn, and how *they* feel about what they're doing, the more reality there is. Also, outside standards are a help— district standards, state standards, national achievement tests. Instead of making me frantic, they actually help me to set certain limits on what I'm expected to accomplish.

And talking to other teachers, reflecting . . . *if* I get the chance to do that. But I'll tell you, I think that one of the biggest things that contributes to my burn-out at our school right now is the progression that I see over time that makes reflection more difficult. When there were just two of us teaching there, Jennifer and I got a lot of time to reflect on the educational process and the kids. We did a lot more talking together. As more and more teachers get added in, and there are more and more responsibilities and obligations to fulfill and kids to deal with and specialization in what we are doing, there's less and less of that conversation. We still have lots of communication among the teachers, but it's more harried. There's so much more going on. There are so many fronts you want to keep together that you don't at the end of the day just kick back with the other person you're working with and yak. You have to spend fifteen minutes with this person, and then you've got a meeting with that person, and so-and-so needs this done by tomorrow.

The teachers—and the parents—aren't giving each other the kind of support I'd like to see. I think everybody is just trying to tough it out and keep it together themselves, but it's obvious that there is just not as much support as we all could use.

As the school gets bigger, our priorities seem to change. At least mine have, although I'm not entirely happy with the change. The kids that are in my class now have a situation that's more organized and clearly defined, and perhaps more suited to their individual needs, but not necessarily as emotionally nurturing or comfortable or pleasant. Efficiency is at the forefront, and humanity is not quite as strong. They're keeping up with their skill levels so they'll be able to pass their achievement tests, and they're satisfying their contracts, et cetera, et cetera. I'm moving them right along. From the outside, that makes it seem like my teaching is successful. Hasn't society decided on the side of efficiency and expediency and the acquisition of "more"—more skills, more knowledge?

For myself, I don't feel that it's that successful—in terms of my original goals. I feel more a tool of this other energy and less a person who's actually creating a good situation. I feel more like I'm implementing, as opposed to creating.

This change—it makes me feel almost cynical. It's the cynicism of the American education machine. The kids come in one door and they go out the other and you just put in the pipe on the assembly line as it comes by. And then there's the inability of the individual to do differently. You might have your ideals and you might be in one of the best teaching situations in the entire world, which in fact our school could be. But still your power to buck the standard expectations is limited.

Sage Looney

middle school music teacher, out of work

Originally, I had no personal interest or no desire to teach, but at the becking of my father, who thought that a woman needs to support herself these days. . . . He said that he would not pay for my college education unless I got something to do that he thought I could make money at. I was a music major in college, and I just wanted to perform and sing and pursue a career in music. But I went along with him and started taking education courses. I figured it was a safety-type thing, and I didn't even visualize that I was actually going to do it.

My first year I was put into a ghetto school, a Catholic school in Washington, D.C., that didn't have any music program. I had all grades, one through eight, in one day. There were three first-grade classrooms, about sixty or seventy kids, all thrown into an auditorium with a seven-second echo. I was *the* music teacher there. I had to use as many resources as I could come up with to handle that.

After doing something like that and pulling it off, I felt like I could handle almost anything. I moved to Massachusetts, where I taught in a few different situations. Some of the schools there, they were kind of short on teachers. Jobs were tight, you were supposed to feel privileged to have a job— so it was just expected for everyone to have a whole lot of kids in their class. That was the attitude that was perpetrated. I guess I did feel lucky to have any job at all. I accepted it, and I just tried to accommodate the kids. So I came up with some ideas for working with larger groups, but I know that my teaching wasn't half as effective as it could have been with smaller groups.

During each week, I had about eight hundred pupils in my classes. The amount of pupil-teacher interactions . . . you could have just in one day maybe over a thousand conversations with different students and different people. Besides just teaching music, that would involve study halls with kids that were not even kids that I knew. There were behavioral room things; there was lunch room duty. I would have about twenty minutes to eat my lunch. I had two different locations at opposite ends of the building, and I had to run from one to the other. The whole logistics of just trying to get my body through the day. I had very little time to do things like go to the bathroom. I developed a few kidney infections that year, just trying to make it to the bathroom. Certain human functions that teachers have to do just like all other people were totally ignored.

I saw each of my eight hundred students once a week, or sometimes twice. The first thing I had to do was learn each student's name. I'm still amazed that I did that successfully. It took me about one grading period, two or three months. But sometimes a name would come up on the computer card, and I was completely stumped. I was expected to give them a grade for classwork and a grade for conduct and a grade for effort, but I couldn't even relate the name to the face. When situations come up like that, you don't feel incompetent, but you do feel frustrated. You want to be able to give each child the chance, but you simply can't. It's a total overload.

In another situation I had two middle schools, and I was the only music teacher. That was another case of overloading the teacher. I had one school for two days a week and the other school for three days a week. There were something like six hundred students in one school and seven or eight hundred students in the other school. I had about thirteen hundred students a week, kids in the sixth, seventh, and eighth grades.

It would take me . . . say, for example, I gave out a one-page worksheet, maybe a listening thing where students would have to fill in the blanks to lyrics that they were listening to on headsets. In order to correct something like that, it would take me about sixteen hours. A simple, one-page thing. The kids, it'd probably take them twenty minutes, but I'd have to sit down for sixteen hours to correct it properly. The pile would be about two feet high. It's outrageous. And you'd try to explain this to the principal. They'd come up with things like: "Don't you have any more time to do this club or that club after school?"

A lot of my frustration, too, was due to the fact that I would have kids who were required to take music classes, especially junior high school kids, who really didn't want to be there. There are three types of kids: the type that wants to be there and has an interest (that's the smaller percentage), then the child who will just go along and be there because that's what's required of him, and then there's the child who has absolutely no interest and who vehemently doesn't want to be there. You have all three of these types in the same class. In music, there's no tracking for knowledge. You might have a student in your class who's had ten years of piano lessons and is totally bored, and right next to them in the same class is someone who has absolutely no background at all. There was never any consideration of where the students were at in terms of the subject, like you might have in math class or English class.

During that time, my teaching wasn't terribly linked to my real interest in music. When I taught the students, I had to be on a whole other level. I kept up on a professional level: I would sing in oratorial societies, and I had a soloist job for two or three years in a cathedral. I did classical music and some opera. But I had very little time to develop my own personal expression in music, because my work load was overwhelming. My day consisted of waking up at five o'clock or five-thirty in the morning. I had an hour to commute to work, and an hour commute back, which was also taxing. Sometimes I wouldn't get home until seven or eight at night. I was married at the time, and there were the demands of making dinner and keeping the wash done. Then there was the correcting of the papers, and a little time thrown in for relaxation whenever I could find it. It was hard to balance it all. It took its tolls in many ways: on my relationship with my mate at the time, and on my own personal health, too.

Aside from that, there was the whole contemporary thing where kids are exposed to a lot of troublesome experiences for their age. Amazing things would come up. I don't know whether it's because music brings out the emotions or what, but I would have to deal with more than just the subject of music. Most of the time I felt like I was a part-time child psychologist, a part-time emotional consultant. I'd have girls consulting me on whether or not they should get abortions at twelve and thirteen years old. I had twelve- and thirteen-year-old boys dealing cocaine to other junior high students. I had boys coming up to me and asking me about their sexual insecurities, whether this was right or that was right. I felt that I had to deal upfront with those kids as best as I could at the time, but I didn't feel like I got much support out of the administration I was dealing with. For example, I consulted some administrators about the cocaine problem among the twelve-year-olds in the school. Their attitude was: "We should just cover it up. We don't want the parents to know about this." I ran into a few situations just by being upfront and open and saying what I really felt about things that were threatening to the administration, because I was willing to be honest and wanted to deal with the real thing, and they wanted to deal more with the politics of the situation.

I found myself getting involved with the students' problems because I just couldn't bear to see such good energy go down the tubes so unnecessarily. I felt like I shouldn't get this involved with the kids, but there I was getting this involved. I had struggles with what level of care you can put out with that amount of students.

My last job, it was an upper-echelon community, quite wealthy. That's where the money was, and that's where the cocaine was. Most of the students owned a sailboat, but it was also quite alarming: there had been seven suicides among junior high kids within the last five or six years. There were kids there that had four different sets of parents before they were age twelve. It most definitely affected them. Teaching those children was probably the most difficult teaching I ever did. They had everything they could want on the material plane, but on the emotional plane and on the spiritual level they were quite undernourished.

It was emotionally exhausting for me. But I never got to the point where I saw a couple of other teachers get to: freaking out, or crying and breaking down in the classroom, or having to take weeks of time off. When a teacher breaks down and starts crying, or when a teacher loses control to the point where they swear at the kids. . . . Another music teacher who I knew actually kicked a boy right in the shins and actually hurt him. This was two days before he quit teaching for good. He had taught for seven years in that school. Teachers just lose it sometimes. It's an unpleasant experience for the teacher as well as the student.

Myself, the work pulled at me emotionally inside and made me feel emotions that were paradoxical. On the one hand, I'd really want to have more energy and put more energy into my teaching, but on the other hand I felt: "I already put a lot of energy into it, and I don't have that much left to give, and where am I going to get it from?" It was a real hard balancing act to carry off. And yet people used to say to me: "Teaching, what a cush job. You only have to work until two or three o'clock in the afternoon." That's a common misconception people have, that teaching is such a cush job. You just have to laugh when you hear it, because you know it not to be true.

One of the hardest things for me was to get up and lecture to a large group of students. I felt depersonalized. I did almost anything to avoid it. I'd break up the class into smaller groups whenever I could. I tried to have maybe four different things happening at the same time. Or I tried to have part of the time set up for the whole group of students, but then the rest of the time I would go around and deal with the kids on an individual basis, talk to them personally. But time is certainly a factor. You can't talk to everybody within a forty-five minute block of time. You're going to run short. And you run into problems like when you're dealing with one student on a project, there's always going to be someone else who's trying to distract or fool around. It's a matter of balancing energies, of trying as best you can to get to each student. That's pretty ideal; it doesn't always happen.

All the different needs of the kids . . . it creates a tension, and it wears you out. I would feel very, very exhausted at the end of the day—and I'm a pretty high energy person. From the minute I got into school, I'd start percolating. In those days I used to drink coffee, and there were days when I would drink five or six cups of coffee just to keep myself geared up for it all. Rushing here, rushing there. Trying to match energies with adolescent kids is at best a difficult job.

And the adults didn't give me much help. The support systems for teachers need a lot of improvement, at least in the public school systems. After having six classes in one day, the requirement is to go to a teachers' meeting and sit there and listen to a bunch of teachers bellyaching about this or that. Or just hearing a bunch of talk that you're not particularly interested in at the moment, but you're required to be there. Then you still have your hour commute home, and you still have to do your own human functions like eat and prepare meals and do the dishes. Then after that you have to get your clothes ready for the next day and get your class preparations done and try to correct a few papers. There just isn't enough time in the day.

I don't know why administrators can't understand that. They're not very sensitive to the real needs of the teachers. The relationship between teachers and administrators, in my experience, isn't that great. Teachers are fearful of administrators, because they feel: "This is the person that evaluates me. I don't want to show any sign of weakness. I don't want to show that I'm fallible in any way." But teachers need to come to the point where they can be honest with administrators and not fearful about losing their jobs. If administrators could just experience the schedules that some teachers have and the particular situation. . . . Also, I think that the parents, the whole community, need to be more sensitized as to what actually goes on in classrooms, what actually is expected of the teacher, and what the hours are all about, not just the eight o'clock-to-two routine: the planning time, the time spent correcting papers, the time spent dealing with students outside the classroom.

When I think back on it, it's hard to believe that I really did all those things without going totally crazy. And I might still be doing it all today if I hadn't moved to Arizona to be with the man I was married to at the time. I was certified in Massachusetts, and I wanted to teach again in Arizona. I already had a master's degree and several years of experience in all these difficult situations, yet I had to go back and take U.S. History and Arizona Constitution and math and a science class, undergraduate courses, just to be able to teach music in Arizona. I started to do it, but it felt like, well, you might as well go back to the little league before you can teach. It really gapped out my professional career, having to go back and take those courses. I was also going through some personal changes at the time, and I finally gave it up. I haven't taught since then. Actually, I'm real thankful for those silly courses, because I'm not sure I would have had the courage to quit teaching on my own.

Where I'm at right now is I'm expecting a baby, and I'm really glad I'm not teaching. I don't think I could be pregnant and carry off that physical task and teach at the same time. Teaching is too demanding a career. I think the wisest decision I've made is to leave teaching for a few years. Possibly when I get back to it, I'll have the right energy to give. My hopes are to be able to teach again, maybe in a private school or on some other level where I can focus more constructive energy on the individual kids.

Steve Adams *fourteenth year, high school English*

A teacher at the deepest level is teaching himself or herself, and not a particular subject. What you're doing, in a way, is giving kids a kind of a role model, although I don't like that term at all. That's especially important here at Westley. The adult male models around here tend to be people who spend an inordinate amount of time at the Hilltop drinking beer. They tend to have fairly unimaginative lives. They tend to be pretty dull people. And the kids know that. They talk about that. That's Westley. Of course, it's often used as an excuse for not doing anything. But I think the kids need people, male and female, as role models who can show them that there are other things—not to put down what they are now, not to make them feel less than they are, but to give them some shots at other things. I try to set up a situation at school where kids can investigate their own creativity. I'm not a romantic, particularly. I don't think that every kid comes down the pipe trailing gilded pearls from heaven. On the other hand, if there's any reason at all for kids to be in school other than the basics, it's to learn how to explore some of their own creative aspects in terms of theater, miming, writing, painting, and all those other sorts of things.

When I first got this job, I told the principal that a teacher should be willing to put a hundred and five percent into his work all the time—and if he's not, he shouldn't be teaching. There are too many people in teaching who might as well be selling shoes. I think teaching is too important a job to deal with that way.

Lately, it's been harder for me to sustain that idea. Just on the basis of personal honesty, it gets to be a real moral dilemma with myself: can I really keep doing this? With some types of kids in some of my classes, I think I do a good job— but there are definitely people who are fresher that could do it better. We're into a very strange year at Westley. Some of the kids, their fathers are in jail. Half the class, their fathers are alcoholics. Broken homes or no home at all. It lends an odd sort of atmosphere to the school.

In some respects it's starting to be a "job," which I really don't think it should be. It should be fun. Sometimes it still is fun. I've got a group of kids coming over to my house at six-thirty to rehearse a play we'll be putting on in three weeks. We'll be doing that till nine or ten o'clock at night. It's really fun. But it's not just play—I mean, they're learning a lot of real important things. When the kids have the energy for it, I am perfectly willing to spend most of the night working on something that's important to them and important to me. There are no stops on how much time I'm prepared to spend with somebody that's into it.

And there are no stops to how deeply I can get into the kids. Every Friday in my advanced placement class we do a free-writing paper. Last Friday the topic was: "When honesty hurts." One of the girls is going through a religious crisis now, so there's this heavy sort of thing for her. Another one of the girls two weeks ago attempted suicide, and is dealing with that not only personally but vis-à-vis her family. Those are some heavy, meaningful, serious things. But I took a chance with those kids. I told them exactly what I thought about what they did and how they were treating what they did and what their attitudes were. I might have been presuming a little bit, but it worked. You've got to take chances, or you never get anywhere.

I gave those kids a hundred and five percent. But I can't do that all the time. One of my ideals used to be, and I think it's typical of beginning teachers, that I'm going to reach *all* these kids. It's bullshit. You can't do that. If you think you can do it, you're kidding yourself. You're in for stress and heart problems and all sorts of stuff.

It's an educational lie that you can group X number of . . . you can't even group two kids together. In simple fact, they aren't the same. You've got a class with some kid that's a virtual parsnip, and in the same class you've got another kid who is a very sensitive, creative, seeking, striving kind of kid. You somehow have to adapt what you're doing to both of them. If you think you can do it with the same book, you're a better teacher than I am.

What I've done for my personal survival—and I'm not sure it's a stance I'm happy with—is I try to identify for myself the kids who I think will repay my energy. Those are the ones I go after. Quite honestly, the rest of them can go fish. However, I'll bet you twenty dollars that there's not a kid in school that could tell you who those kids are. Some of them are obvious, but some of them aren't. Maybe that's only my rationalization, but even if you sat in on my class for a week or two, I'll bet you couldn't tell who I was trying to concentrate on and who I wasn't.

I don't think I'm going to be teaching here next year. I don't think it makes any sense. We have a very capable group of seniors; they've been a really wonderful group of kids all the way through school. And there were a lot of kids in front of them that were very worthwhile students. I'm not making any personal judgments, in terms of "This person should be shot" (although that might be a good use for a few of them). I'm talking about kids that either are or aren't interested in learning anything, that are tappable in any way. After this year's senior class, there aren't many left that are tappable for about five or six years. We have a large mix of kids heading through that high school now who are in and out of jail, who are suspended from school (some of them three or four times already this year—and this is only the eleventh week of school), who don't want to be here, who don't have any other skills. I mean they couldn't be anywhere else. In essence, they're being institutionalized in school to keep them off the streets. They know it, I know it, everybody knows it. But I'm not a cop. If I wanted to be a cop, I'd be a cop—not a teacher. I don't want to be one of the wardens in the institution. I simply don't want to do that. I won't do that.

I've got classes where there's maybe a couple of kids who want to learn anything and the rest of them. . . . Take my second period, for instance: it's a literature class of seventeen kids. I decided: "I've been shining that literature class on for too many semesters; I'm really going to make something out of it this year." It's a lot of work to do that, but I put together a reading program that involved some short stories, a novel or two, and so on. I know that most of the kids in there are not going to go to college or anything, but I figured I could reach them somehow. Well, I found that on a given day I'd assign a paper overnight, and out of seventeen kids, three kids would turn it in. With that kind of payoff, I finally said, "This is ridiculous! I am going through all the hassle of doing this; I'm assigning all of these books, so I've got to read them too. Class, if you don't want to do anything, that's fine. But this is a school. You come in here, you don't want to do anything, you don't pass. I'll put you on individual contracts. If you want to read a book, I'll give you a paper assignment for it. If you do enough to get an A, I'll give you an A. You can get an A in this class or you can get an F in this class.

The only thing I insist on is that you don't make much noise, because there are some people who are trying to work in here—and I'm going to use this class to prepare for some other classes where kids want to work." So that's where we are. That's the way I'm running that class for the rest of the semester. And the funny thing about it is: it doesn't bother the kids. There are two or three kids in there that are doing very well. They're using it. The class is a good class for them, because what could be better, if you like to read, than to have a place where every day you could go for forty-five minutes and sit quietly and read? It's great for them. And for the other kids, they don't do anything—and I don't care. I've got too many other kids in other classes that do want to do something, that do want to work, for me to spend my time on kids that don't.

Maybe I'm overstating how I'm not dealing with them. I know their names, I take work from them, I grade it, and so on. All that normal stuff is done. But I'm not going to waste time preparing lessons that I have to do much research for. It's just not worth it.

In some of my classes, I feel it's me against them. That's largely why I'm not liking the job. I have the feeling that I'm the old English teacher that comes in here and tells you, "You gotta do this, you gotta do that." I don't have anything in common with them at all. I don't like that attitude in myself. I don't like that self-image. I'd rather be siding with the kids. I'd prefer to have the feeling that I'm waging guerrilla warfare against the establishment down there. My allegiance shouldn't be to the school, to the parents, or to anybody else—just to those kids. That's who I'm here to work with.

Even though I'm having my problems, in some respects I'd rather be working with the Westley kids than with suburban kids. The suburban kids are just not very interesting people. They're cooperative, and they're behaved. They dress nicely. Their fathers aren't alcoholics, and few of them are in jail, but they're not very interesting either. That's one of the things I like about this place: the people. I mean, they might be drinking beer at the Hilltop, but that's a step above sitting in front of the TV every night. It's still got a bit of the Wild West. It's a place where people can be who they are and not have to worry too much about what the guy down the road thinks about it. It's the real world. Of course, that's what creates the problems, because when those people also happen to be uneducated, alcoholic slobs whose only interest in their kids is that they're not home all day because they send them down to school, that's not a very pleasant situation. It's the underbelly of the place.

Teaching in Westley has two aspects to it. Partly, it's like being in the Peace Corps, or like being in a VISTA school on some Indian reservation somewhere in North Dakota. And it's also like being in a real school—a regular public school just like every other school everywhere.

Actually, I've been very proud to be associated with this school. I think it's a good school. In some respects, I think it's a better school than the town wants it to be. A lot of people in town want the school just to be a place to babysit the kids: "Don't hassle us with rules and regulations and grade point averages and requirements that they pass anything or do any work. We pay our taxes. Just take the kids, and let's leave it at that."

I like schools. I think schools can be one of the highest manifestations of civilization. And I like to teach. I like to teach when the kids like to learn. I don't mean to indicate that I can only relate to a class that's got a bunch of panting scholars that are lusting after every single word I say. But I like to teach the kids who have a fairly good attitude, who are nice people, who are kids who you'd like to spend some time with. Not kids who you're afraid to turn your back on. Those kids are reachable, I think—but they're not reachable by me.

Even if I had the classes now that I had when I first started teaching, classes with lots of interested students, I think I'd still be getting a little impatient. But that's good, too. I mean, the president can only work two terms; I think teachers should be the same way. Let them do something else for awhile, then they can come back to it later if they really want to. I'm overstating it and being a little flippant, but I don't think that people should feel that their profession is what they're locked into until they climb into the grave.

I want to preserve my good feelings about what I'm doing, but it's harder to do that now than it's been in the past. I want to get out while the getting's good, while I still feel good about myself. I went through this last year. I went to the middle of May. I gave myself a date—May 15—to make up my mind whether I'd come back. I think I made a mistake—sort of—by coming back. This year, God knows I may change my mind yet as it gets closer to May, but from where we're sitting now on the twenty-second of November, I don't think I need to be there.

Actually, I've been playing this game for five or six years.

Each year I think is my last. I don't necessarily envision not being a teacher. If I could find the right job under the right circumstances and the right place to live, I would even move to be a teacher. But if the right job is not out there, I could stay here and not teach. I could take my retirement out. I could pay every bill we owe and still have ten grand. That's a nice place to be. It wouldn't last long, but there are other things I could do to make money. It's not like you never make another dime again.

I could write a lot more than I'm writing right now. Of course, there's plenty of starving writers in the world, but at least there's some potential for money there. I could coach baseball. I could substitute at school. I could do a junior college drama class, and get paid for that. I could grow dope. I could do a lot of things. It's a free country. It's America, right?

I'm pursuing some other things. I'm talking to the College Board people down in Palo Alto about the possibility of doing some consulting work for them, which would be a little money. Or it might be interesting to teach in a private school for awhile, a college prep. I've even had serious discussions about starting a private school right here.

I know these are hard times, but I cannot believe that my family or myself will suffer severe hardship. Maybe that's just a function of my eternal naiveté. But we'll own our house—that's an important one, right there. We'll own our car. We know people. I think we have the ability to get by.

I don't look down on people who feel more trapped by their jobs. I can understand it. But I think it's a self-defeating attitude. When teachers start to think about their jobs as something they do to make a living, it's bad news. It's easy for teachers to just maintain and go along—*if* they don't care. If you don't care about what's happening to the kids and what's happening to the school, you're just collecting a paycheck. You might as well be selling vacuum cleaners. It really doesn't matter. If you care, it becomes very difficult.

When teachers over a long period of time don't care, don't care, don't care, when they just maintain, they should be thrown out. It should be easier to fire teachers. That's my union position. The problem there is: who gets to do it? I mean, teachers are bad enough; administrators are real turkeys. A person who is maybe a good teacher ends up being an administrator, and sooner or later they reach a level where they can't function anymore and they tend to stay there. An administrator, a principal, should be a leader. It's a position where a person should be able to do more than just count paper clips and sort the mail. That, unfortunately, is what principals seem to do more often than not.

Personally, I refuse to look at teaching as a way to make money. I don't want to come home every day (and it isn't every day, but it is a lot of days now) feeling like I've just done something that I basically don't like to do: I've been around a bunch of people I don't like to be around, I've had to enforce rules I don't like to enforce, *ad nauseam*. That's not fair to my family. It's not fair to me. And it's not fair to those kids, whether they deserve it or not, because I'm not giving them anything. So it's not fair to anybody. The only justification for doing it is because they're paying me a bunch of money because I'm willing to do it. That's not enough, if I want to maintain any good feeling about education. There's a potential for real cynicism there, if you're doing it just for money. It's like doctors talking about dead people.

My impatience with this job is a gradual sort of a thing. There's no critical event that happened, like you'd see in a play. It wasn't anything like that. For a long time, I just thought that I went to college and I got my credentials and I got a job and I'm a teacher and I like where I live and that's what I'm doing. So that's what I did. After about nine or ten years of doing that. . . . My kids were starting to grow up. I'd been here for nine or ten years, and anybody that lives anywhere for that long starts thinking: "Am I really where I want to stay?" About four or five years ago I was safely past thirty and heading fast toward forty, and there's that business to think about too. You only have one life, right?

I'm not exactly scared by time, but it is a mild concern. If I didn't start into my midlife crisis about four years ago, it was a real good imitation of it. It's terrible. I have a very dear friend in Sacramento that's literally on the verge of suicide— largely because he's forty years old. It's stupid, but it's true. You start looking: "I'm going to be an old man before I get very much further on." When I get self-reflective (which doesn't happen very much, particularly when school's going on), I take inventory, and I think I've done a number of things that were useful. I don't feel bad about not doing anything. On the other hand, I think there's the potential for doing a lot of things that I can't do if I keep doing this.

There's a world of possibilities out there. It's a childlike feeling of trying something on for size and let's see what happens. My personal experience has always been that whatever our plans are, life is usually even stranger than our wildest fantasies. So let's see what happens next.

David Reynolds

It was really going to Mexico that got my head-space shifted. We got a sabbatical for a year and traveled all around Mexico. Then I had to come back and go back to work. I was just about to turn forty, and here I was going back to the same old job.

During the year I had been away, I made lists of things I'd like to do with my life. All kinds of things. One of the ideas I had was a mobile natural history bus. I could go around from place to place and work with the kids, or the adults. I wanted to keep some of that mobility I had during the year in Mexico, and not be tied down to a single job. I also thought maybe I could get into carpentry. Then I thought I'd investigate other types of work, things like the Sierra Club or Friends of the Earth—jobs where I'd be dealing with adults, and not dealing with kids.

When I've worked with adults . . . we have these explain-your-courses-to-the-parents nights, and the parents always say: "Wow! I wish I could take that course myself." They would be ideal people to have in my classes. Get these housewives who don't have too much to do, and they're really eager to learn. I thought it would be fun to work on that level, to get a job where I could explain the need for preservation from a natural history point of view.

You get frustrated with kids. You're always dealing with the same problems. Kids never seem to grasp photosynthesis. Even though I've taught it to them for a dozen years, they still don't understand it. There are all these new kids, but they're all in the same place. They always have the same problems in understanding photosynthesis. After a while you really begin to wonder why you're doing this over and over again.

Also, one of the things that gets to me is just adolescence. High school is a hard age to work with kids, because they're

not that interested in school. They're *beginning* to get the
capability of doing some sustained work and to develop intellectual curiosity—but they're not quite there. They're much
more concerned about who they are, how sexy they are, and
all this sort of stuff. So you're sort of beating on them all the
time. They go along with it, but they don't really like biology
that much.

And you want them to be liking it. I'd like my students to
get a feeling that the natural world is interesting: when they
go somewhere on a family outing, that they pay attention to
what's going on around them. In a sense, that's my major
goal—the wonder of nature. I feel good if I can just get them
to appreciate how fascinating and complex and beautiful it
all is. But another part of me feels that they should learn a
lot of stupid facts. That's put on me by society, by the university people. I've been trained in biology, and I'm supposed
to pass that bundle of stuff on.

Sometimes I get too concerned about how they're pro-
ceeding academically. I get too heavy with them, too serious,
and that takes a lot of the joy out of it. Then if I back off,
things get too loose. I flip-flop back and forth between being
too tight, too organized, and too loose, too unorganized. It's
a no-win situation. I'm damned if I do and damned if I don't.
And whenever I'm doing it one way, I'm wondering whether
I should be doing it the other way. There's always reason for
getting down on myself for not doing it right.

Anyway, I taught for that year, but it was pretty chaotic.
From a distance, I had been pretty excited about teaching
again. My course descriptions were great. I was all inspired.
I had been living out-of-doors for a year. I was going to get
those kids out into nature. Then school started, and they're
just the usual mope-a-dope kids. "Eh, do we *have* to do that?"
It was just too hard to go back to work after having that year
off. Finally I said, "To hell with it. I don't have to do this
anymore." So at the end of the year I quit. I turned forty
years old in May; by June I was out on my own.

That next year was extraordinarily frustrating. I'm one of
those people who's very day-to-day. It's hard for me to get
going with long range planning. So it just went along. September went by, October went by. Winter came on, and I
began to get more uptight about it. I had a lot of uncertainty:
"What am I doing? Where am I going?" I started working on
our buildings. That went real slow. Then I got some jobs
working on other people's houses. I had a great deal of trouble
with estimating costs. I'd make a bid on a job, and then I'm
such a perfectionist that I'd put in many hours of time beyond

what I was getting paid for, to get the details just right. I wasn't very efficient.

That year was a bomb, a terrible bomb. I tried to get naturalist jobs at all these places, but it didn't work out. I almost got on with the Nature Conservancy, but that didn't go. I wasn't very diligent about pushing myself. I did a resumé that I sent around, and I talked to people, but I didn't really follow up with lots of phone calls and get very pushy. Meanwhile, I was farting around with the carpentry stuff. Also, I had thoughts about getting some kind of business going with nature, but I didn't really get into it. I was fiddling around with some photography ideas, too. I was doing a little bit of this and a little bit of that, and trying to apply for those jobs, but I wasn't doing anything *well*. I felt a terrific and increasing pressure from my wife to get something going: "Here you've been out of school for three months, and what have you *done?*" She has a much more straightforward approach: "Just organize your life and get *going.*"

Also, I started drinking real heavily, trying to numb out a lot of this anxiety. I'd be out on these carpentry jobs, and it was lonely up there. I learned right away that I was a people person. I'd been in the classroom; I'd always had colleagues, people around. Community High is a place where you have social time with people, time out of the classroom. It's not like one class, another class, another class. You have breaks, you have long lunches. You're always talking to people. You're not always getting a lot done, but you're having a full, interpersonal contact.

So here I am in these empty houses, banging away in basements, all by myself. That kind of work goes real slow—sanding wall board and all that stuff. So I started drinking on the job. I'd listen to the latest news coming up every hour, the same news over and over. I'd try to put the music stations on, but I'd get bored with that because it's all rock and roll. So I'd go back to the news stations and hear it all again. My work would slow down even more—it seemed to take *forever.*

Then in the spring we decided to go skiing, and I tore my knee apart. That did it. There I was in a cast from my hip to my toe. I had to sit around in the living room and sort slides. I had these stacks of boxes of slides—all sorts of beautiful pictures of nature. It was the only thing I was capable of doing. I drank while I was doing that, too. So then the slides were sorted, and now they're still all sitting around, just the way I left them, with all the little rubber bands around them.

By the end of that year, I was ready to run back into teaching. I had my tail between my legs, although I tried to cover it up as best I could. I went to part-time to get back in, because that was all they had available. I did some administration, too. Gradually, I picked up my old teaching load. But I was running behind. I didn't feel on top of it at all. I was drinking pretty regularly. I was having a hard time doing my school-work. I wasn't doing the stuff I needed to do. I wasn't getting my papers graded; I wasn't getting the laboratory set up on time. I'd go in cold every day, and a little bit hung over.

The guilt was never-ending. I carried a big load of shit around with me all the time. I'd carry my pack back and forth to school every day with all these books and papers. It was symbolic. It was just my *load*. I put more stuff in there than I could do in a week, and I carried it all home. Then in the morning, maybe without ever looking at it at all, I'd carry it back. I carried it everywhere I went. If I added up all the pounds, and that could be translated into some kind of re-ward. . . .

Since I was never adequately prepared, the only way I got by was to be an entertainer. I'd just start talking, and whatever came out was the lesson for the day. The entertainer number is the easiest way to bluff your way through. There are a lot of teachers who do it; some of them do it very well, and are considered popular teachers. It's just like watching TV. The kids sit there and watch it for an hour, then shut it off and go to the next class.

For the next couple of years, I bluffed my way through like that. I did the best I could. How many years was it? God, I can't keep track. Anyway, this last year I had a real crisis with alcohol. I dropped out in the middle of my spring course. I went into the hospital for a month to dry out. It's an Al-coholics Anonymous program. I'm still in it. I go to meetings three times a week. You never really get cured of alcohol-ism—it's just one day at a time. But the days add up, and I've been straight for almost a year.

Now, I'm in another place with my teaching. Just being straight makes a whole new approach. Kicking alcohol is like going through a religious conversion. I've had to look at what I'm doing, and I've had to deal with it on a daily basis. It's working. I like it. I'm able to remember things. I have a lot more continuity from day to day. I develop the subjects more logically, and students respond to that. Now, I'm not trying to please them so much; I'm trying to get them to think and learn.

I'm not so concerned with being popular anymore. I guess a lot of teachers have to go from being a young, popular teacher to being an old fuddy-duddy. I've been undergoing that transition, and I'm very aware of it. Before I took that year in Mexico, I'd always try to engage their interest through some of their own channels. They'd all go out on field trips and appreciate nature stoned; they'd get real excited about it that way. In this loaded state, they could focus on the far-out things in nature. I used some of those tools. I had been attractive to the girls, and I'd use that one. You can get everyone's attention that way.

There's nothing basically wrong with being a young, energetic teacher with time and energy to spend with the kids. I could tell a lot of old war stories from my younger days. We really had some high times. We fixed up an old school bus and took a load of kids down into the desert, driving on dirt roads without even a track. Really, there was no road at all—and there we were in our school bus. We just had adventure after adventure on that trip. We spent weeks on beaches, deserts, mountains. We were really out there—Lewis, myself, and a group of students. You couldn't go away from the group and do your own thing, because there was nothing out there. I mean people were *afraid*. You're two hundred miles out there in the desert, two hundred miles from anything. No Mexicans, no towns, nothing. Two hundred miles to the next hacienda.

That was a wonderful trip. Then there were all those trips to the Southwest, Death Valley, all the California studies trips. Then there were the demonstration days, when we used to go with the kids to demonstrate against Chairman Ky. And the ecological days, when the kids were so active cleaning up beaches and stuff. I would come and unlock the doors to the school, and the students would run these meetings. There were kids there from junior high schools and high schools all over town. On their own time, they'd come over in the evenings and organize ecological action projects. All I'd do was . . . I was like a visiting expert. I'd give them factual information when they asked for it. They did the rest. People really wanted to learn, and to use what they were learning. So it was fun being hip and slightly cool—a young, over-committed teacher.

There's a real place, an absolute need, for that groovy teacher like I used to be. It's a valuable role. But for me, at some point, it became an inappropriate role. As I was getting older, I couldn't relate to the kids on their level as well. I didn't want to. I wasn't interested in what they were interested in. So teaching was becoming increasingly difficult. I was finding a lot of failure in my relations with students; it just wasn't working in those other ways that used to work. Some of the teaching magic, or whatever it was that I had with the students, wasn't there. I grasped that intellectually; I knew my age was forcing me into a transition.

I knew I was getting older when I'd look at the parents. The students always stay the same age—but their parents seem to get younger. I used to look at parents from a kid's point of view. I was very sympathetic with the kids. I'd cover for them with parents. Then gradually I came to the point where I was the same age as the parents. I would talk to them on an up-front, person-to-person level: "I have kids the same age as yours." Now, I'm slightly older than lots of the parents. I talk to them as a mentor, as an older teacher who's been around.

As I was getting older, I started to think: "Do I want to be a *teacher*? An old teacher, sitting around school with dandruff on my jacket and having everybody snicker at me behind my back? Do I want to end up in that place? Or do I want to go out into the world and make a name for myself?" I really struggled with that one. I never really solved it, but I just decided: "What the hell, I like what I'm doing. We'll see what happens." As you get older, as you cross forty and see how things are going, it doesn't seem to matter so much. You begin to realize that what you're doing is okay—*if* you're enjoying your life, which I am.

Now, I don't feel that same urge for fame and professional advancement. As a matter of fact, I had some opportunities in administration-type work, which is often thought to be an advancement. I was co-admissions officer for a year, and I worked on special admissions for a couple of years. I did well at that, and I felt good about it, but I was essentially a salesman for Community High. I'd much rather sell nature than Community High. I mean, Community High is okay, but I just can't develop the same kind of enthusiasm for a school as I can about nature.

I didn't really like that work. I did in some ways, because I could dress up, put on my suit and tie, look very preppy, and go out and talk to a lot of good-looking mothers. I could be in that whole role. "He talks good," people said. I was dealing with adults, and they were appreciative. Then Community got to fooling around with having a dean of boys, and word was that I was going to be approached for that position. Boy, I steered away from that. What a horrible job, to be in charge of discipline. I don't view that as an advanced position over teaching.

I'm not tempted anymore to leave the classroom. I really

like teaching again. I'm in a new position with the kids. My goal is still the same, but I go about it differently. I'm not an entertainer anymore. Instead of lecturing to them about photosynthesis, I have them read and write about it first. Then we discuss it in a way where they have to look at it from around fifteen points of view. I just keep shifting grounds on them, so they really have to think and put it together. How are the plants which grow in the aquarium under a light bulb using solar power? They have to reason all the way back from the power plant to the fossil fuels and to the age of the sun. Thinking that through is a lot harder than sitting back and being entertained.

My whole attitude toward students has changed. I can see them more for who they are without having to impress them personally. Going through this alcohol thing has helped me gain a perspective on things. Now, I really value my daily human contacts with students, as well as with colleagues. I focus my energy more on them. I force myself to concentrate on the fact that: "There is Joe. I'm talking to him. He's talking to me. I'm listening to him." Those kinds of interactions have regained their value and meaning. I find a lot of what the kids are up to fun. I'm not trying to share it with them the way I used to, but it's just plain fun to observe and talk and interact with them. I feel more relaxed with this perspective.

Also, I feel like I'm growing again. I'm learning. Rather than just dredging up these old talks, I'm approaching things differently myself. I'm reading more in my field. I'm preparing more for the courses. I'm developing new techniques. Even though I'm familiar with the materials, there's always new ways to go about it. I'm learning a terrific amount about native plants and birds and all kinds of other things I'm interested in. I learn a lot of this right in my classes, by observation on my field trips. Just today, I ran across a couple of new pond creatures. When I find something that I'm really excited about and that's new to me, the students get excited, too.

I want all my students to get turned on by biology. I don't want anybody in that class just to be sitting there taking the course for credit. They catch on to that. Even if they're not interested, they damn well look interested. Either they get excited about things in that microscrope, or I'll nail them: "What are you doing sitting around? Look at something. There's all these beautiful things to look at." I get messianic about it. I want them to get the message—and to become little missionaries themselves. I want them to turn their own kids onto it. It's all how much energy you put out. If they see in you someone who is totally mesmerized and captivated and enthralled by the subject, that you really have taken the trouble to learn, and that you *still* are excited about stuff that you've been seeing for a long time, then something of that enthusiasm rubs off on them.

For me, biology is so incredibly fascinating in a way that other subjects aren't. Biology is every day, every moment. It's my avocation and vocation. When I'm walking around, I'm looking at it and I'm thinking about it. It's the major focus of my life. I'd be bored silly if I wasn't into biology. No matter where you go, the world is there. I guess for some people there's a lot of sociological stuff: different cultures, architecture, paintings. But biology is *everywhere.* You don't have to go to a museum to see some paintings. You just go for a walk.

sixteenth year, fourth and fifth grades # Frances Marinara

I didn't have a driving force, a passionate desire, to be a teacher. I wasn't on a crusade. I just happened to fall into it. I was looking around for a role. I tried to emulate people, other teachers. I thought this is what I should do. But the role wasn't fitting, and I was feeling very strange, very out of place. I had no sense of what I was doing. After three weeks, I said to my principal that I was bored and frustrated, and that I'd really like to leave teaching.

But my principal seemed to feel that I could do the job. He said. "Give it more time." So I stuck with it. In the first few years I grew to love the children, but I still felt I was just playing a role: dressing a certain way, acting a certain way. About my fifth year I started coming out of this role. We had a new principal, Frank, and he supported all the things that I'd been hiding for years. I started teaching not from something I had learned in a book; I started to develop my own style. I started looking inside *myself*.

When you're with children, you learn a lot about yourself. Why do you feel this way? Where is this coming from? There's an openness in teaching. I've been teaching for sixteen years, and it's still helping me grow. It keeps me asking, "Why am I doing this? What need is there in me? Why does that kid bother me? What is it that I see in myself?" It gives me a background for looking at myself, and that may be what keeps it so alive and active for me.

Teaching is not just a one-way thing. It looks like, "She's got these kids that really love her." But I really love them, too. Maybe it's because I don't have my own children. They're about the only kids in my life, except for a few friends of mine and my niece and nephew. I find children basically more stimulating than adults. I want to be around them. I want them in my life.

The last day of school, when people are so excited, I'm one of the most depressed women. You've got this family for nine months. It's like a pregnancy. Then all of a sudden you have this child and you have to give it up. It's very hard for me. I get scared by the amount of time that's not structured. But I'm more used to it now. It hasn't been quite so hard for the past five or six years. Now, I don't need children as much as I did to make my life function. I have enough of a social life. But the kids are a very creative part of my life. I don't mean "creative" just in an artistic sense. I mean I'm doing, I'm acting, I'm being. I'm not dead. They force me to not get old. They force me to really look at them.

I enjoy the whole process of being with these minds that are clicking, and being a part of it, making them curious. Today I started reading *Frankenstein* to them, so they can appreciate that he wasn't just this jerk on TV, that he's somebody to love and pity. I got more excitement out of *Frankenstein*. . . . I'm so excited tomorrow to go in and read the rest of it. Kids come in with a black-and-white; they want justice, they want everything just right. I'm saying, "No. Life is not always that easy."

What I like to do is make children feel uncomfortable. They come to school with this idea that they sit like dummies or like marines in line, and they think that that makes a good student. Those are their expectations, and I want to change them. I want to make them feel uncomfortable with those traditional roles, because that's the only way they'll ever look at themselves. They come to school saying, "Everything should be fair." And it isn't. Even though they're only in the fourth or fifth grade, they live with it already. They live with just as real situations as you and I do. They live with parents who are poor—or rich. I have kids who come from places that you and I would never venture to, where they live with guns or hatchets in their houses for protection. So I should tell them that life is fair? Today, we're not any longer dealing with children whose life is a fairy tale. They live in the real world. For me to make them think that life is fair all the time, that you're going to get what you give, is bullshit.

Children have to be treated like people, not like they're four years old or seven years old or ten years old. You don't have to wait until they're in college for them to start thinking about things. Children are so knowledgeable about everything: about finances, about sex, about movies, about violence, about love. You're dealing with, in many ways, adults. If you negate that part of it and make them think that school is just reading, writing, and arithmetic—negating the music in their life, the hate in their life, the violence in their life, the love in their life—it's negating a great part of them.

I share as much as I possibly can with them about my own life. I share my ups and downs. I share my weekends with them. They know I love to dance, I like to go out to dinner and see films. My kids call me at home all the time. I don't know if this is good or if this is bad—but I need to do it. It's getting children to feel like there's a family going on, and we have to care for each other—because I think that's the only way we'll make it.

It's basic to me and my needs—not necessarily something that *should* be. For me, it makes it worth it all. It makes me keep wanting to go tomorrow. It's a family for me. It's a place for me to give and get. I'm not just a giver. No way. I get *a lot*—probably more than I'm giving. We deal in this honest way. Sometimes I have to remind myself that they're only nine years old, and they're still in the developmental process. But no matter how old they are, you have to contact children on the emotional level.

For the past three years, the kids line up before leaving school and I kiss them all good-bye. I know other people look at us, and they think it's phony bullshit. But I need it, and I know they love it. The first time I did it I thought, "Are they going to be repelled by it?" I've got Vietnamese, Chinese— children from all over the world. It makes me realize even more that if something is real, it's so universal. You break down cultural barriers. Vietnamese kids who've just come over, boat people—I kiss them every day.

What's happened in education is . . . just the words, "Loving you," you're not supposed to say this to children. I'm almost embarrassed by it, embarrassed that I kiss them, when there's people watching. I mean, I'm the only teacher I know that does this. There's such a lack of people showing feelings to kids. They think that they, being the teacher, should be this disciplinary figure that doesn't emote, either anger or love. You always have to be in control.

That's the key word: "control." The easiest thing in the world is to say: "All fold your arms. If you don't do this, you don't get six points. Good kids stand in line. Ten points for you." I can see the temptation of it. You get order right away. At times, I wish that I had that—but I couldn't live with it. Teaching for me is dealing with individuals, not puppets. Taking time, stopping, and listening to them. Taking the time that has nothing to do with what you have planned, which sometimes can screw up your whole day. Like taking care of a kid's ripped coat, which I did the other day.

It's like going to a cocktail party every day, and you're the hostess. You have to deal with everybody—not just as a group, but as individuals. I mean, they all have different minds, different needs. It's like being the director of the symphony. You're trying to cue in to everybody—which is sometimes an impossible task. You've got to know that this kid feels bad, that kid feels another way, and so on. It's always keeping on top of things. You say something to one kid, it works; you say the same thing to another kid, it doesn't. I have different goals for different kids. For one kid, he needs to work harder; for another kid, maybe she's working too hard. She's too serious. She's trying to please. What she needs is more joking around. She needs to be allowed to screw off. But I can't encourage the rest of the class to screw off. So it's a juggling act. That's what makes teaching hard for me. It's emotionally exhausting.

I'm still in doubt. If you're a grocery man or a garbage man, after sixteen years you have a lot of confidence. It doesn't go that way with teaching. You go up and down and up and down and up and down. People think, "Sixteen years at a job, you should have it down cold." Maybe so—if you treat every kid the same, and if you use the same lesson plan every year. But you've got a different class, a different make-up. And from year to year, you change. Lately, I've got a lot more guts, because I'm thinking I might get out of it anyway. So I'm at this point of thinking, "Fuck it."

A few years ago, things started going downhill. Frank, my principal, got ill. He wasn't at the school much. Eventually, he died. Friends of mine were asked to leave the school—not by Frank, but by the people who took his place. There used to be four of us who felt about the same way about things. We used to give each other support. Now, I'm the only one left. The only support system that I have are my parents. I'm still excited about teaching, but the support system is no longer there. I'm wondering: "Is it worth it for me to continue?" It's really hard for me to do this alone. Children give you a lot, but they demand a lot, too. When you don't have a support system, that's hard—because you're always doubting. No matter how secure you are, when you have the rest of the faculty acting in a different way. . . .

It would be very hard for me to go to school now if it wasn't for the children. I miss them when I'm not there, but I don't miss the staff that's around me. I isolate myself, because I can't relate to them when they talk about teaching. We talk a different language. It wasn't like that when my friends were still there. They offered an alternative. That's what Frank did: he built a community school where various alternatives were offered. There was a power struggle within the faculty, but Frank was saying: "Do your thing. I don't believe that one class is better than another class, but let's just give the community a choice." The school was *alive*. It gave parents a sense of community, a sense of power. Now, I have to remind parents that they do have power. That's very sad.

The community school idea was okay for a while, but the teachers began being threatened. A lot of the classes I had were filled with parent requests. The other teachers didn't like that. They thought that kids who were in my class from parent requests were easier to deal with. That kind of petty resentment started a lot of tension, and it might have caused some of Frank's illness. He tried to please so many people. That was interpreted as "losing power." It was. He was giving up a certain power to the community.

People have said to me, "If you have such strong feelings about it, if you liked what Frank did for the school, then why don't you become a principal yourself?" That would destroy me. Because of what's coming down on you, a principal is faced with the paperwork. No matter what your goals, it will kill you. My principal now makes a choice. It's easier for that man, who's going to retire soon, not to buck anything, to be safe, to fall back on his paperwork—because his personality is more toward paper. He has never looked (and I'm not being poetic or dramatic) into the eyes of any child. He just listens to words. That's why kids weird him out and have a lot of power, because he never looks into their eyes to find out where this is coming from.

Let me tell you a story to show you where his heart is really at. I've just gone through the worst two weeks of my entire life. I didn't envision my life to go this way, as far as my father was concerned. Two major operations—if they didn't do them he would have died. He has arteriosclerosis all over his body. All the vessels are closed up except one, and they had to clean out that one with like a roto-rooter kind of system.

Then my cousin, who was very close to me, was busted. Then the day I bring my dad home from the hospital, and I don't even know how long he has to live, my uncle is found in the water—and he died the next day.

So this has all happened within about two weeks, and everybody knows it at school. The day I'm to pick up my dad, I get a letter (which I keep, just to remind myself of what I'm dealing with) from my principal. It reads:

Frances, I know your dad is topmost in your mind, but there's a bulletin board to do when you get time.

This is the second day I'm back to work. I get this letter in my box right when I'm leaving for the hospital. I would never think of doing this to a child. You know, "Your mom just died, but did you do your homework?" I thought, "My God, what am I doing here? What is this all about? Our goals, our ideals, what we're here for, are so different!"

I was absolutely devastated by this letter. Yesterday I was asked to do it again. My friends, the people I used to work with, couldn't even believe it. They said, "I'll come in for an hour and do your bulletin board." Because they know I have report cards due, I have two weeks of papers to do— plus coming back to my children and dealing with them. They've been without me for two weeks. This is the first time I've been out that long in sixteen years.

My kids, when I came back to school, they had a big surprise party for me. They brought me two big bottles of wine and had cookies and cake and ice cream and everything. They made these big elaborate signs. They're loving the fact that I've come back. They had even washed the floors, because they know that I like a neat setting.

When I was out, the kids needed to know how I was doing. A few kids would call me every night, wanting to know how my dad was. Then the thing happened with my uncle. The kids knew about that, too. I told them, "I don't think I'll have to leave you." But I did have to leave school an hour early, because my mother fell to pieces. An hour after her husband comes home from the hospital, she hears about her brother.

I think the kids have the right to know these things about me. If we want to establish an honest relationship, they've got to know what's happening in my life. There are certain things that I keep secret, but I share most of what I do with them. And they do with me, too. Like I want to know what they do on the weekends. I want to know what they do when they get home.

A kid that I had last year called me last night, the second time, from Louisiana. I said to myself, "I'm just embarrassed. Why is this kid in Louisiana, who is not rich, calling me up?" Of course I get a kick out of it, but what is it? It says there's something that's valuable. I don't know if a lot of other teachers think it's valuable. And I'm not sure if what

I'm doing with the kids is really any better than what they're doing. I don't want to sound like an elitist. All I know is the kids come back and they remember me—for whatever that's worth.

I don't know if I could get along without these kids. I've never done it. All I've ever done is taught, so I'm really naive. I may be very unhappy without them. But in the past few years, I've started to think seriously about quitting my job. Teaching has become much more psychologically demanding. You've got all these other things, all this paperwork. Many principals believe that these things are very, very important—more important than dealing with children. They pay lip service to the children, but they don't really care. Most administrators, they know nothing about kids. There's a disconnection. They've been out of the classroom for years, and they simply don't understand children. But they do understand paperwork. It's not education—it's big business and a lot of pressure.

Profile cards are the worst. You have to test children on these various skills. They have them in English, math, and language. If they pass the skill by this particular test, you check it off. They are cards that nobody looks at the next year, but they are cards that downtown feels are important. If this particular child's skill has been checked off, they can say that the child has the skill in hand. And you're supposed to have these cards on hand in case some bigwig from downtown comes by. You're even supposed to memorize them: you're supposed to know right away if some child has this skill, if he's passed this test. But the profile cards, and the tests that they give, and the way you check them off, don't really tell you if the child is equipped with the skill. If you test him one day, he might get it; if you test him the next day, he might not. So what you're being forced to do is to fill out cards that nobody looks at, that nobody really respects, that they don't consider accurate—but you're still forced to do them.

This takes up an energy that should be given to children and to the whole learning process. I'm forced to do this kind of thing in the after-hours, because I'm not going to give up time filling in a profile card when I should be there with the kids. At night I come home and I've got their stories to read—but I don't mind that, because there's a real connection with the children. With these profile cards, there's no connection. The same thing with report cards. Report cards tell a parent very little about what's happening. It's the same kind of structure as a profile card, and they don't allow for much else.

What I see happening in education is that these outside expectations are getting to be more onerous. I see teachers doing these bureaucratic chores, and they hate it. They consider it phony, but they do it—because if they don't do it, they get called down by it. It all starts at the top. If the top guy says that's important, and that's his priority, then you're going to do it. So what am I going to do? I can't say, "To hell with it. It's not important." I'll say to myself, "I can't do it during school time, but I'd better get it in. That's what that guy expects."

The only way I can deal on this level is to not be associated with it, to deal with the bigwigs as little as possible. And yet I have to be aware of what's going on, because I have to do work in this school. The thing that I try to do is to block it out. I don't challenge it directly. Once you get into trying to buck it, you're getting into a whole other thing. That's where you get teachers who are so political, so into the union, that they have to leave teaching—because they put all their energy into politics. I choose not to put my energy into politics. If I did, it would have to be all of my energy—and where would I be with the kids? So I just put my energy into trying to be who I am.

The pressures that I have on my job, children become the victims of it. When I'm in a high-pressure situation, as I have been with this particular principal, I bring the pressure into the classroom. I've got conflicting expectations, my own and his. That puts me in a stress situation, and it's bound to rub off on my teaching. That's what makes teaching hard for me. You feel like you're never doing enough, because you're dealing with those other expectations from the people around you—people who don't even know your world. If I do leave teaching, it will be because these outside expectations, which do not mean anything to me, wear so much on me that they take up too much of my space, and I can't give as much to the children. I won't be able to deal with what I think is important.

If I quit, what I would do is probably work at a restaurant. I like restaurants because I like dealing with people. There's a service involved. I'm getting something back—not so much tips, but an exchange. I know I'd like that, dealing with other adults who have that same feeling of maybe owning a restaurant, having another family spirit of making people feel at home in our restaurant. It's a long-lasting dream I've had for seven or eight years. Whether this will happen, I don't know. How long I'm going to be in teaching, I don't know.

Last year I said, "This is my last year." Then I come into contact with the group of kids I have this year, and they're giving me a lot. So I'm thinking, "Maybe another year." I don't know. All I know is I love these kids, and I love being their teacher.

Frances
Marinara

Helen McKenna

twenty-first year, high school science

Teaching is like running a marathon. You work into a long, steady stride, day in and day out. I've got a rhythm going. I party and play and relax on the weekends, and yet I *really* work all week. I live hard. I do get tired, because it's too big a job. The way the system in the schools has been set up, the poor little mice can never run fast enough. That's us, me and you, the teachers.

But there's no point getting hung up on the oppression of it. It's written about and talked about, but it ain't gonna change—because of politics. There's no way that the powers-that-be are going to give us the time and the money to do the job right. That's what burns people out. Five classes a day, five days a week, thirty kids in a class, and all the other responsibilities. No money, no respect, no T.A.'s, no secretaries, no coffee machines, no phones, no paper. They give me an hour a day to administer the department. That's a joke. And they're always talking about taking it away: "Really, you don't need it. You can fit it in somehow."

So why do we do it? Why do we let them run us around the track? You have to be an advocate of what it is you're teaching. To be effective, you have to have something to say about whatever discipline it is that you're in. If you're a math teacher, you should have an advocacy for mathematics or numbers or logical conceptualization. If you're an art teacher, you should have an advocacy for the love of art. For me, I'm into the outdoors, the environment, and critical thinking and critical judgment vis-à-vis science. And also having a good time. So that's what I'm working on in my teaching.

I'm really challenged by creative things to do within the constraints of the system. But the minute you get into difficulty is when you don't recognize what the constraints of the system are. You can't change it. In this kind of institution I'm working in, you're not going to change the bell schedule, you're not going to change the room arrangement, you're not going to change the students that you get. So the problem is trying to figure out how to do some things within the constraints of that structure that feed into what I want to advocate.

The best kind of environmental science program would not be meeting fifty minutes a day, every period. But in order to reach a lot of kids and have an environmental class at all, that's the way it has to be. You've got to plug it in, just like you plug in chemistry and physics and biology. You've got to use that format.

Sometimes you can bend the system around to some extent. We tried some flexible scheduling at a time when the powers-that-be were ready to hear about flexible scheduling. We tried some curriculum reform when the climate was right to try curriculum reform. But I never have gone out on the edge for something unless I knew there was some energy around to support it among the superiors. This computer thing I'm doing now, I *knew* that it was how we were going to go, and I sat down and wrote the proposal and I was able to get all the people behind me. I knew I could make it acceptable to the system.

Your first responsibility is to the kids—not to the politics of running a school. I like to think that everybody that's been in my class has had a change in themselves as a result. It may be very small, but they're changed. They have another view of the biological world, another view of the environment, another view of science, another view of women in science. And maybe another view of themselves.

But over the years, the kids change. Like right now the kids are politically less interested in getting out there. They don't want to do all the things that kids wanted to do ten years ago. Then it was easier for teachers like me to work with them, because they were ready to hear me and ready to do all these things. Now, I don't have as many expectations about what they're going to do with what they learn. That's important: not to expect too much. These are fifteen- and sixteen-year-old kids, and I try to remember periodically my own feelings at fifteen and sixteen. Then I'm surprised at how much my students *are* doing—when I compare it with myself at that age, and all the kids I knew.

I was totally interested in parties and social things with boys. I was in all-girl schools that were very, very rigid. Catholic schools, with some excellent teachers who were totally dedicated to their work. They weren't all good, but they were dedicated. They got up early in the morning; they worked all day. Their whole life was their teaching. They were a teaching order of Sisters which was founded back in the sixteenth century just to teach. I went to school with these women for twelve years.

I guess some of that dedication rubbed off on me. "If you're going to do a job, then do it well." "The life of the mind is more important." All that stuff—I was rebelling against them, but I still believed it. I don't mean to say that I'm totally into personal sacrifice. I don't have a martyr complex—although I'm frequently one of the last cars out of the parking lot, if you want to use that one. I've asked some of my teacher friends: "Well, what do you do that's so interesting at three o'clock?" They throw their hands up at me. I mean, some of them go home and watch the soap operas. Sure, there are a lot of people who are not pulling their weight. But when you work in a big school like mine, you can't waste your energy about what the people on the second floor are doing. The only time you bother to worry about it is when somebody gets knifed in the room, or something really major occurs as a result of some incompetent person.

You have to put in a lot of time to do a good job. That's going to be true in whatever you do. Good teachers have to like their work. They don't have to be saints; they're not giving up anything. As a matter of fact, they're living—living in a real and full way that a lot of other people aren't living who are supposedly not saints. All you have basically at the end of the day is: "What did you do today?" If you've done your job, you can feel good about that. You're fulfilled.

Basically, I'm fulfilled by my work. If you take it day by day, you almost can't miss. You go in and out of it, but most of the time I'm satisfied.

Of course I do get bored. After four or five years teaching the same class, even with new students and new ideas, it starts feeling routine. So what I've done is I keep introducing new courses, or changing courses in the curriculum. And now that I'm in charge of the department, there's no problem at all to do that—because I'm the one that authorizes these changes.

I do still have the counselors to deal with. They have their own ideas of how the curriculum should be structured, and they assign the students according to their ideas. But I tend to work fine with all levels of kids. When I have the real slow kids, I do okay with them. When I have the middle kids, I do okay with them. Now I've done what most department heads do: I have mostly the good kids to work with, because I do more okay with them. And they do fine with me.

The slow kids . . . you have to remove yourself. You can't take it too personally. Because if you have a large class, and there's one or two who aren't catching on, you can help them a little bit, but you can't do a whole lot. For one thing, I'm real busy. My day, from the minute I walk in the door to when I leave, I've got a lot of responsibilities and assignments and meetings and things to do. I don't have the time to say to a student, "You really would profit by coming in for an hour's worth of tutoring." Because I can't give it to them. I don't just forget about them. I try to ask them questions and give them ideas and encourage them and praise them when they do something well and team them up with other students who can help them. But a lot of times they end up with D's. It's hard to teach everybody at once, the bright kids and the slow kids.

The adults, too—you can't please everybody at once. Everybody has their own ideas of how to run a school. I don't have much trouble with that—I just think I'm right. If I think I'm right, if I feel good about myself, I can handle it. And even if people don't agree with me, I'm protected. I have tenure, I have a union, I have a reputation, I have support from people I've worked with in the past.

Every year I think seriously about quitting. There's this natural thing: the term is going to come to an end, and maybe I'll go out and look for something else to do next year. But then for one reason or another some grant moneys appear or some project comes up and I say, "Well, I'll just come back for one more year to do this project." Last year, for example, I got this grant from the state to do an endangered plant trail in the Arboretum. I'm really hot to do the project, and I've committed myself to the people at the Arboretum to do it. I don't want to not do it. So I'm back. Something like this always seems to come up. I make it come up, and then there's a reason for me to come back to work. I've been playing this game for the past ten years, but I haven't recognized it as a game yet. Each time I tell myself that this is my last year, I really mean it.

If I did quit teaching, I'm not really sure what else I'd get involved in. What are you going to do in society that's meaningful? And I do believe in meaningful work. Working with the kids in the public schools is a very meaningful job in our society. One of the only ones.

And yet it's terribly difficult. The kids are ungrateful. They moan if you give them homework. They clap if you tell them you're going to be absent. And they act up—things like a student taking a squirt gun out of her purse and squirting the kid in front of her while the class is working. Or hollering out, "What's the cure for herpes? Extra-strength Tylenol!" I'm giving you specific examples from my sixth period class this week. Writing on the tables. One girl, I asked her a problem and she walked out the back door—not to come back. These kids have been in school eleven years; they know what's right or wrong in the classroom.

I know these behaviors from my own student days. I've done most of that: sneaking out of the room when the teacher was on the phone, calling out the jokes, the squirt gun. None of it seems that *bad*. With these kids, I'm sympathetic to them—but I also have to deal with them, because you have to have the establishment of order if you want to teach. People have different definitions of order. One guy might want all the chairs in a row and one sheet of paper out and they raise their hands every time. That's one definition; somebody else's may be different. But you have to have some definition of what the order is. The word *discipline*—some of the liberals in teaching look on it as a bad word. It shouldn't be. Discipline is an integral part of the teacher's role. Of course you have to have back-up staff; the teacher obviously can't do it alone. If you have a kid who is disrupting the classroom, you've got to have the support of the bigger structure of the school and the community.

My principal supports me. He also gives me a lot of compliments. And the other teachers, the people in my department, are terrifically supportive. I need that kind of positive feedback. My husband, my friends, my children, my parents, my brother—they all give me strokes for my work. And my students when they're grown-up. I run into them and they always tell me how they really remembered that class and how important it was to them and how it changed their ideas. Or they're at college, and they say, "You know, we're doing a lot of the same things we did in your class." And even the kids now. Some of them say, "This is the only class I look forward to coming into every day." Those strokes really help. On the other hand, I hurt when the students don't want to be in my class. It really gets to me when someone transfers out or tells their counselor they don't like the class. But that's the way it goes. Not everybody is always going to like you and what you're doing. Especially when you're an advocate. When you're advocating things, some people aren't going to agree with you. Whereas if you were bland and didn't have a position . . . well, they don't like you then either. You can't win for losing with this thing. You can't be so good that everybody thinks you're good. You can't be good about everything.

I have my weaknesses. Sometimes I think maybe I'm losing it, losing whatever gift I have. I get to the point where I never want to see another paper again. There's something terribly tiresome about correcting errors on papers year after year after year after year. If you're going to help a young person improve, you have to point out their mistakes. So I do it. Even though it's a science paper, I circle all the misspelled words. If you can't spell, it's like raising a red flag: "I'm not educated." They have to know what they missed. Teachers have that responsibility when they're given a piece of writing—they have to respond to it. I don't mark the students down for grammatical mistakes, but they do have to be notified. So I read them all. I read them fast. I have to be fast or I couldn't survive.

When I went back East to grade the essays for the College Board people, I had one of the highest outputs. I'm one of the fastest readers in the country. I just know how to do it. I know what to look for. I know what all the answers are on the paper. And I know what all the wrong answers are going to be.

I've got a week's worth of papers at home. There are sixty lab reports from two sections of one class. Then there's sixty five-page reports from the same class. These kids had to write a five-page report and a lab report last week. The lab reports are about a page and a half each. So I guess that's about four hundred pages from that class. Then I have a set of quizzes for a class that's very small, only fifteen. And another set of papers from a class of thirty. And they had a test on Monday which I already corrected. That was sixty tests. So that makes about five hundred pages this week. It'll take me about four hours to correct this stack of papers, to circle the mistakes and put numbers on them and record them in my book.

The kids need this feedback. They use it. I can see it in their growth. They learn how to do a lab report and how to write a paper. In science there's a particular kind of writing you're going for: what's the purpose of what you're doing, did you do it, what did you find out? There's a format there that forces them into certain ways of thinking. What did you plan to do, what happened, and what does that mean? What's the difference between an observation and an inference? How limited is observation? What proof do you have for that thing you believe in? These are life skills that go beyond science. If you can solve problems in science, you can begin solving problems in society and in your own life. It's the old "science is the answer" school—I'm still bought into it.

That's why I'm a good science teacher: I believe in it. Although, like I say, I have my weaknesses. I'm not real good at getting my students to follow up on their individual interests and pursue their individual projects. I tend to just go through the course outline. And I don't have the time to have the after-school science program where kids will come in to work on things, which is really useful. There's no question that in science teaching there's a real need for that kind of stuff. But because of my family and my own time demands, I just don't do it. The problem is: the job is infinitely elastic. You've got to do it *all*. Of course you can't do it all, so you wind up drawing the line. Different people draw the line at different places. It doesn't matter where you draw it—you always feel you should be doing more.

It's a matter of survival—that's why you draw the line. If you want to keep working for twenty years, you learn to set your limits. Twenty years . . . among the peer group that I'm in, it's unusual for people to start a job at twenty-one and still be there when they're forty-one. So I'm unusual, but I also get bored with it, just like anybody else. I get bored with the place, the physical place. It's not a very beautiful place. It's not a nice environment to be in. I don't like being indoors all the time, and yet I'm at a job where I'm indoors *so* much. I'd really like to be outdoors more of the time. Maybe not even out of doors—just out of being in the same *room*. I was in one room, and then when I got promoted to department head, I switched rooms so I could be next to the office. But it's exactly the same as the other room, so I've been in the same room for twenty years, every day from eight o'clock until three o'clock, teaching about science and the great outdoors.

But I'm also really interested in people. I don't want to be outside wandering around all day all by myself like John Muir. There's an incredible parade of people that comes through Washington High—and I love it. The kids teach you a terrific amount. And that's what's fun, when there are so many things that come the other way. All kinds of things— big things, funny things—that you can get from a class of thirty people from all these parts of the world and all the different cultures.

So I do get a lot out of this environment, in terms of the people aspect. I may just stay here and keep working with these kids for twenty more years. That's okay, I could do it. I've come to better terms with that. But I'm in a period right now where I'm also thinking about doing something other than what I'm doing. I've come into contact with a young assistant principal, a woman, that I've really enjoyed working with. She's taught me a lot about counseling, working with people, my own approach—how it has its positive and negative aspects. I enjoy working with her on administrative problems. In my department I've found that it's a real challenge not only to be responsible for what goes on in my classroom, but to encourage other people in my department to improve what's going on in their classrooms, to provide the materials and the positive feedback and even sometimes the negative feedback that they need to hear. That's been interesting, but it's really hard to influence how other people teach.

If I go into administration, that would be my goal: to improve teaching in other people's classrooms. That seems like a funny thing to do if I'm not going to be teaching myself. I'd like to see an administrative job where I could teach one or two classes in the morning and work on administrative work the rest of the day. That would be my goal. I really don't want to get out of the classroom totally.

There's always a lot of challenge in the classroom, but I'm looking for a new type of challenge. I'm looking for more like a frontier. Computers are a frontier for me. I'm working on a big project, opening a computer center in our school. We've been able to raise a lot of money and get a lot of support from people all the way at the top. There's a lot invested in making this work. Computers are like books—a whole other tool that's going to be available for education. I want to see how we can best use that tool.

For me, seeking new frontiers is tied up with ambition. Being around a lot of higher-uppers that are ambitious tends to make me more ambitious. I say to myself: "I play this game real well." There's an urge to compete, to get the kind of praise that you get when you're running more of the show. I'm thinking about ambition a lot.

Somebody said to me that I was a very powerful person at the school. I was surprised, because I didn't think I was powerful. But then I decided that a powerful person was one who had ideas they wanted to implement. So then I was powerful, because I do have a lot of ideas, and I have implemented a lot of them. In the sense that ambition is a function of wanting to see your ideas in practice, I'm ambitious. And I'm looking for power.

Part of the very nature of teaching is power. A teacher is doing that with the students: wishing to transmit some ideas to them, and get them going on it. If you want to advocate something, you have to accept power on some level.

Of course there's a psychological aspect to ambition. My whole life, my brother has always been seven years older than I am—and very successful. He's one of the top two or three people in the world in virus research. He's world class. It's a hard act to follow. Even in college I was ambitious, but the climate for women in scientific research in 1962 was not good. If I had gone into research, it would have been on a very low level. I didn't want to work in somebody else's lab and be the dishwasher lab lady. Teaching seemed more promising. Also, I had this idea that with teaching I could go out and change the world: get all these young minds and influence them, and the world was going to change. There were tons of offers in teaching at that time, and the pay was good. No problem for women to get a job there. So I decided about two-thirds of the way through college to get my teaching credential. That was it; I didn't have to worry about a career anymore.

I went into it, and it was easy from the very beginning. Everything was fun. I knew I was okay. Everyone I worked with said I was okay. The students said I was okay. The people who were running the show were very supportive of me. I was encouraged. It would be crazy to leave that, when you start out doing it well.

I had one experience leaving, when I went up to the University of Oregon on a year-long fellowship to get a master's degree. They really wanted me to stay and get a Ph.D., but I was at that period getting very cocky about how we were going to change the world, and we certainly weren't going to change the world doing research. This was in the late sixties. There were so many social problems in the cities, and I was going to go back there and deal with all those problems. The action was in the high school; it wasn't in college doing research on frogs.

So I turned the offer down. It was a good offer, too, but I didn't have any trouble turning it down. Probably I *should* have had trouble, now that I look back at it. I should have thought about it a little bit more. But I was very know-it-all. That's one of my problems: I *do* think I know it all, at the particular place that I am. It's only later on when I look back that I realize I didn't know it all.

That's another one of my weaknesses in teaching. You can sometimes turn off students with that. And it can be a problem with your colleagues, too. So I'm trying to work on listening to other people, and asking for criticism—and being able to take it. That's hard, but it's really useful. This is new for me. It's another frontier, like computers. But probably harder.

For this frontier I have to move out of the classroom, because the students can't do much of that. The person you ask to give you criticism has to be fairly powerful, or they won't give it to you. The students don't have that power, and they're not articulate in that respect. They may know there's something there, but it'd be very hard for them to tell you. They're experiencing you in a very limited relationship. And they're into accepting you on that level: "This is Mrs. McKenna, and this is her act." They're not going to question that, unless what I do is totally unfair.

So I have to be around adults more if I want to get more into feedback and the development of my own personality. Maybe that's why I like all these new projects. I say to myself, "Why am I getting involved in these committees? I've got all these other things to do. I've got five hundred papers waiting for me at home." But I take it on, partly just to be working with other adults.

The "Quality Circle" is particularly important for me now. It's an opportunity for me to grow. Because of my science background, I tend to focus on content—all science people tend to be this way. And I'm very restless with process. The Quality Circle is the first project that I've had a lot of respect for that involves process, and making me understand it. I'm really beginning to see that a good idea, the process by which it develops, is as important as the idea itself. There are nine million meetings a day in America. Teachers spend at least one year of their lives in meetings. Yet how do you feel when you leave most meetings? I'm interested in how it is, if I'm in those meetings, that I can facilitate and participate so that everyone feels better when they leave the meeting, and that the meeting's process is apparent to people as well as its content. It wasn't just that this was a meeting about chairs, but this meeting went such and such a way because these methods were used, or not used.

I've been hired and trained as a facilitator at our school for two Quality Circles made up of groups of interested teachers who want to work on a problem within the school structure that they think they can solve. I've been instructed in ways of working with people in a group, encouraging them and otherwise facilitating their work. I'm dealing with the group process, and I'm real excited about it. I want to make it work. Yet it may not work. We may or may not be able to function.

Annie Waugh

twenty-fourth year, first and second grades

I can't imagine anyone going through life without goals, without a direction. Ever since the sixth grade, I went directly for a teaching credential. All through high school, I knew exactly what I was going to do. It amazes me, people being twenty-four years old and out of college and not knowing what they're going to do with life. My, how aimless. How lost they must be. I can't even relate to it.

I went right on through and became a teacher. It was everything . . . it *is* everything I wanted it to be. I can't imagine doing anything else. I can't imagine any other job. I love working with the kids. I enjoy the rewards: seeing them grow, seeing them respond, seeing them become independent for the first time, hearing a child read that couldn't read the first of the year, seeing a child say all of a sudden, "Oh, I get it!" There's something every day if you take time to think it over and think about the positive things, and don't dwell on the negative things. If you get down in the teachers' room with "Oh, it was a hell of a day," you can get into a negative feedback, but if you stop and say, "Okay, what was *good* about my day? What *did* occur?"—there's always someone that has made some growth in something that has been a delight.

I'll get caught up like everyone else in the teachers' room. Sometimes it feels good to go down there and just blow off, but when you get into it too often and you get into negativism there, it's time to readjust your thinking. I'll catch myself and I'll come back and say, "Now wait a minute. Why did you feed on that? Sit down and think. What *has* occurred today? Sure, he was a pill—but what could you have done to stop it if it really bothered you that much? If it was that bad, then it was partly my fault."

After school, I'll sit in here and talk to myself a lot. I'll say "What have I done wrong? What will I do right? What will

I change? Who haven't I spoken to lately? Who haven't I said
something positive to?" I continually ask myself, because if you don't stop and take a couple of minutes a day to think back about your class, about what was good and what was bad, you'll just repeat the bad. You might have sent a kid home with a negative feeling about himself because you didn't say something positive that day. If I feel that I have neglected a person, then the next morning I will try to make sure that I say something positive when they come in: if they have new shoes, if they have a dress on, if their hair is combed. It doesn't take much with children, just to register a nice comment for them.

Children are so honest and open. They'll walk in and they'll say anything to you. They'll give you a hug, or they'll walk up and say, "I'm mad at you today." You relate to these feelings, and try to feed back to them. You feel so many emotions and you go through so much in a day's time; no other job would ever have it. You get angry, you have joy, you have fun, you see accomplishments. The children continually feed you all these emotions, and you feed them back. I like the continual change, the perpetual change. You never know what's coming from one day to the other. You have your lesson plan made out, but it doesn't mean that this is the way it's going to end up. Every day is different.

You have your goals and your objectives and your curriculum. You've laid out what you want to accomplish for the year. You know where you're going, but your interrelations with people are different. I know that I'm not going to come in and stand here and turn a screw every hour for eight hours, and that I have to do twenty an hour. You never know what's going to happen. You don't know when a child is going to come in and be delightful and just bubble over, and that you decide you're going to let this child have sharing—to heck with this part of the curriculum today—because he needs this. Or someone comes in with a tragedy: the dog died. So you immediately change to cope with that. Or they've had a home situation where they're upset, or they come in and they become upset with me, which occurs. Then I decide whether I can change that attitude, or whether I feel that they need to be angry, and that I need to be angry, and that they know we have these feelings. I say, "I know you're angry, but I'm also very upset with you. That doesn't mean I don't like you, but I'm certainly upset with you, very upset with you." If I bottled it in, or they bottled it in, it wouldn't be very good for either one of us.

You always express your feelings with the children. You

don't hesitate to tell them when you're angry or when you're happy. We all react to things; the world isn't made up of people standing over and above emotions. The children must learn to interact on the emotional level. If they don't learn to interact, then they're going to have problems in the future.

Sometimes you react too much to a child. There was one particular girl a few years back that I *really* liked, to the point that it was harmful for her, because I would find that I was favoring her. She and I were too close. I was allowing her to get away with things that she shouldn't. She would turn on the tears. Usually I won't put up with tears for too long, but this particular child would have *me* practically in tears. She was getting away with murder, so we transferred her out. I was very sad over it. The parents didn't want to move her out either, but I insisted that she be transfered to the other classroom. It was not a healthy situation in this class. She was playing me. She had fond feelings for me, but children will play you for all they can get. And she was playing me to a fine fiddle. She had me perfectly tuned.

It goes the other way, too. A child that you have a negative feeling for, there's usually nowhere to transfer him, because there is no other teacher that's willing to take the child. I usually can build up rapport, but there have been instances when I've found it difficult. If I have one that I really clash with, I spend time marking in my lesson plan book: "How many times did I talk to the child today? How many times did I give him positive feedback?" I will make an effort to give that particular person a lot of positive feedback. I work at trying to be aware of how I'm treating him.

I've had some that I just knew, from watching them on the playground, that I wouldn't be able to tolerate. Then they arrive, and once they're in your classroom they're *yours.* You're as protective towards them as if they were yours at home, your own personal ones. "*My* class." It's a possessive thing.

Sometimes your negativeness toward a child isn't really directed toward the child, but toward a particular parent that has been a pain in the kazoo. I've had that occur once or twice, where there was a parent that interfered and was such a problem that you hated to see the child come, because you knew behind the child was the parent that creates all the problems.

I had a delightful child about five years ago, really a wonderful child, but mother came to work in the classroom. Mother didn't come to work to help out the class; she came to help her son, who she felt was very bright and gifted. She spent a lot of time belittling other children, helping her son over others, demanding that something be done this way or that. A very domineering, pushy woman. I found myself continually explaining to her, or trying to pacify her, or giving her jobs to do that would remove her from the classroom. Well, one day I noticed that I hadn't talked to the boy for a week. I'd been avoiding the boy all this time, because his mother was driving me up the wall. It wasn't fair to the child, but it occurs.

Most of the parents aren't like that. You call parents up at any time and they will come. You ask them for bean bags and they'll send them down. They're really helpful—especially in this school district, much more than in the other districts where I've taught. The parents want to help; they want to give their child every advantage they can. And most of them do it in a positive way. I have a woman coming in who is almost deaf and partially blind. I have her daughter in the classroom, who is also visually handicapped and will be deaf. She's getting gradually more hard of hearing. So her mother wants to come in and do signing with the children, and she's doing a delightful job. The children are really quiet and pay a lot of attention. It's working out beautifully.

I have many parents whom I would like to be really close friends to, but I won't allow myself to be. They live in the district, and then if you say something about someone else, if you go home and say to the neighbor lady, "Oh, did I have a day! Johnny drove me up the wall"—well, you would be amazed at what comes back if Johnny's mother hears it. You would have all kinds of problems. This did occur to me about my second year of teaching. I lived in the district where I taught. My neighbor took care of my boys, and I stopped for a cup of coffee with her when I picked my boys up. It wasn't until a couple of months later that I found out I said too much to this woman. It came back through the grapevine and even made it to the administrators. She had really embellished it. Ever since then, I don't like to become friends with people in the district. Once burned . . . I would never again live in the district where I taught, and I have an unlisted number. You'd be amazed by the phone calls you can get, and the hours you get the calls. Eleven o'clock at night: "Johnny told me that he had homework, and he lost it. Can you give me the problems over the phone?" And you're in bed asleep when they called. This happened to me in Brookside when I taught fourth grade.

Now, I choose my friends more carefully. I can confide in them, but most of the time when I have a problem at work or I need support, I either talk to the people on the staff, or if I feel I have to go higher up I will go to Art, whom I feel very free with. He's the administrator here. I'll say, "Hey, I think I may be doing this or doing that. Would you like to come in and observe this lesson and give me some feedback?" Art does a delightful job of that.

I have real open communication with this administrator. The past administrator, no. Many times teachers feel betrayed by their administrators. Teachers as a group can feel the administration has betrayed them because they will go and ask for raises, and the administration will usually not back the raise proposals. It's too bad that teachers have to negotiate for their salaries, because it puts them in conflict with their administrator, who has to make out the budget, but who also supervises their work. It puts him in a very negative role.

It's too bad that there cannot be money raised for schools and decent salaries and supplies and materials, that the public won't support the schools with a positive outlook instead of always pointing to the schools as the bad guys, the one that's created the problems. The public is always screaming that Johnny can't read. Johnny really can read, much better than many years ago. You have so many people coming in with their own ideas of what schools should be teaching: manners, sex education, values clarification, prayer in the schools. Then somebody else comes along and says the schools should just stick to math, reading, and writing. The teacher is caught in the middle of all this. Parents come down and are upset by this or that. Some parents, you can talk it over with them, but some parents can really raise hell. As a teacher, you try to be careful about what you do or say in class. Sometimes it feels like teachers spend more time tiptoeing around certain subjects than teaching them.

It's a very political job, from the pay to what you do in the classroom. You can't escape it. My first job, I taught for several years and then I got into a conflict with the school board. Their wages were among the lowest in the county. The new mandated law came in for raising the pay of teachers. They felt they couldn't do it, but they had a new teacher come in and they payed her the new mandated wages. So after five years of working for them, I was making less than the new teacher. Then they wanted to put in hot lunches. They said, "To hell with the teachers. The kids need the hot lunches more than they need the teachers." So I thought: "Fine. Have your hot lunches. I'm moving on."

My next job, I disliked the administrator violently, and I

disliked the way the school was run. I was there two years
and thought I was going to have a nervous breakdown. There
was power play among teachers, which is really a bad situation. I came in, and there were two fourth-grade teachers:
one had all the good students, twenty-four of them, and I
had all the children who couldn't read or were problems or
disciplines, and I had thirty-two in my class. That doesn't
turn you on right away when you come into a new school.
Then I had one boy who was beaten regularly at home by
his drunken father, and I went to the Welfare. The administration really gave me a bad time on that: "We don't bother
the Welfare with these problems."

The next year they gave me a nonreading class. I had twenty-
five to twenty-eight students, and every time one of them
would start reading they'd move him out to the other class.
They left you holding the rest. I had one boy that came in
that was Indian, and he had an enlarged pupil. I thought,
"Gee, that's odd. They had eye tests last year, but that doesn't
look right." I watched the child, and I noticed he was bending
over just three inches from his paper. So I went down to the
office and asked: "Does so-and-so have a sight problem?"
They said, "Oh, no." I said, "He's only inches from his paper.
I believe he does." They said, "It doesn't matter anyway. His
mother's an Indian. She won't do a damn thing about it."

The next day I went back to the office and said, "I want
the child tested." Meanwhile, I took the child to the chart,
and he couldn't see the big E. I told the office. They said,
"Well, Annie, are you qualified to have that child read the
chart? Have you taken the course?" Any idiot can measure
twenty feet off and have him read the chart.

The nurse showed up the next morning. She ran in and
grabbed the child. I swear she wasn't gone more than five
seconds before she came back in the room. She said, "There's
nothing wrong with this kid's eyesight." Well, I was in a
rage. I went down and pulled his cum records. The child
had failed the eye test in kindergarten. In the first grade there
was a doctor's note saying that he was incapable of reading
the alphabet, therefore they did not give him the eye test. I
flipped it over and looked at his IQ test, and his IQ was a
hundred and fifteen. How high do you need to take one of
those tests? So they had just completely brushed over the
situation. I went ahead and called the parent, and told her
that she had better get that child to an eye doctor. They took
him in the next morning and the child had had amblyopia,
where you need a patch over the eye. He should have started

years ago. Consequently, it was too late, and the child was blind in one eye. It could have been helped, it could have been stopped if it had been caught even the year before, the doctor said. So the parent and the eye doctor came down on the school pretty hard. Well, you know who the school came down on: me, for being a troublemaker. I did not remain at that job for too long.

From there I came to my present job, and I've been here for fourteen years. I probably would have left here five or six years ago, if jobs were available. I didn't particularly like the attitude of the administrator they had at that time. He was very blasé, a PR man: keep everybody happy, but do nothing. Don't rock the boat. That's not my style. We're working with children, with our future generation. We need to have concerns over them. If we don't give a damn, how do we expect them to give a damn when they grow up? If somebody's in this profession, they should be in it for the good of the children. That's what we're here for.

If an administration is really, truly interested in children, then I feel much easier working for them. I feel they're being honest and open with me. I have conflicts with Art to a certain extent on certain things, but he still is a caring man. He cares for the kids, he cares for the school, he cares for the teachers. He wants it to be the best school possible. He's willing to give you feedback. He's willing to help you grow. I need that continual feedback: "You need to try something else, Annie. Why don't you try this or try that?"

That's one of the things I like about having student teachers in my class. They try things that I would not myself do, such as I would not role play. I find that difficult to do, but they come along and do it. They come up with fresh, new ideas that I think will never work, but I'll say, "Go ahead and try it." I'll observe it, and many times it's a slam success. I will learn and pick up methods and grow by having student teachers.

I spend my life working in feedback. I go around and find out from other people whether I've done what I wanted to do. I structure my own positive feedback—then I get upset when I get negative feedback! But without feedback, you become sterile. I've known a teacher who had been teaching for thirty years and was using the same old lesson plan. She never rewrote that lesson plan, and she was proud of it. But your classes vary. Sometimes you have a sharp class, sometimes you have a class that is slower. Sometimes you have a class that has a mind of its own, and they're really strong for a subject or a topic. Then you go that way. If you're going to survive and get along, the children have a little bit of say, too, about what they're going to be taught within the curriculum. How could you use the same lesson plan?

As teachers, we tend to cut our bridges down and isolate ourselves. We have a fear of receiving negative feedback. The public scares us. I find at times the parents scare the hell out of me, especially if you've got a real pushy, gung ho one that wants to raise cain. Then when you get burnt . . . I tend to be one that if I get burnt, I withdraw quickly. Also, with all the negative things that are written up about teachers and schools, if you feed upon it, there's a lot of negativism that can build up. Yet if you retire within and close your doors, you're bottling yourself in. And teachers tend to do that: "Don't hurt me."

Teachers like to control their own class. I've got that domineering streak in me that I shouldn't, but every once in a while I'll want to play the part of the controller. I suppose I do it more than I want to admit that I do it. That is in me, but it's something I try to curb. I'll try to control things at home, too. My husband knows it and will tell me to stop it.

Tom helps me out in a lot of ways, both at home and at school. He'll come over and do things for me. He'll do projects in the classroom: he put the hooks in the ceiling, he put a shelf up for the art, he put in a paper cutter. He comes in and every year he'll do a project for me. Sometimes if there's something that needs to be done over the weekend, he'll come over and help put up bulletin boards and things. He's a stickler for cleanliness; he comes over and washes the windows every year. He takes a real interest in my work.

It's been easier for us since our two boys have gotten older. Tom and I are alone, rambling around in our house. When the boys were younger, we were really poor. It was hard for us. I think the boys suffered by my going off to work; I think I gave more to the job than I did to the children. Thinking back, I would have done it differently. Economically, I don't know if I could have left teaching for a couple of years, but I probably should have stayed home when the boys were younger.

I was carrying my oldest boy when I was still in college, and working at the same time. That was really exhausting. A couple of hours typing or just answering the phone, and I was literally dragged out. Teaching has never been as tiring as that. Of course there are days when I'm absolutely bushed. It's like any other job, you do have your ups and your downs—

but I don't feel worn-out, hate the job, like I never want to come back and see the classroom in the morning. I don't have that feeling.

As it wears on toward summer, I do look forward to summer vacation. I rest up June. By July, I'm starting to think, "What do I want to do next year? How do I want to change it?" By the middle of July, you'll start seeing me down here, looking at my room. Sometimes I'll just walk in and look at the room and walk out and take a book or two home. By August, you will find me here at least twice a week, four or five hours, and getting real excited about it. By September, I can hardly wait. And yet the night before school starts, I have butterflies and I don't sleep. Tom says, "Why don't you ever grow up? My God, you've been doing this for twenty-four years. Why should you be upset and worrried about whether you've got everything?"

Juliet Sherwood

high school chorus, semiretired

I began teaching when my daughters were in cooperative nursery school. I knew I had some feeling for teaching—I certainly loved little kids—so I thought it might help me to do this nursery school work. Eventually, when my kids left the school, I just stayed there and became a regular teacher. I had more and more fun with that job. I got involved in music, because there was a dance man who would come around and needed accompaniment. I did music with whoever was there. I had never done improvising before, but I loved it.

Finally, when my kids were in junior high school, I figured I could take on a heavier teaching load. That was in 1958. I decided it would be a good idea to go back and get my credential. It turned out I had two years of work to do in order to become a music teacher. Well, it was lovely. I loved going to classes. I didn't have any desire to leave.

When I did leave, it was to do the music program in a junior high school. There were a lot of black kids there, angry black kids. This was in the early sixties. I had to learn how to handle it, how to do "confrontation," if you want to call it that—to recognize that these kids were disturbed about something, to bring it out in the open. We'd talk about it. That worked like a charm. People don't stay hostile when they know you really care about what they have to say.

It was one great turnaround for me, but I started having a ball. The previous music teacher just had a ladies' program, because it was harder to get men involved in music at that level. But I started getting boys that wanted to stay in it, so then I had a really great choir of seventy kids that were both boys and girls. It was the only choir of that kind in the city. I took them to festivals, and we'd get rave reviews.

Then I thought it was time for me to get into another group, so I went up to Jefferson High School. I wanted to work with more mature voices and do more difficult music. My objective was to teach the reading of music and a refined vocal sound. I was able to do that. I started reaping the results of my earlier work, because I had a lot of the kids that I had trained in junior high school.

I had classes of up to eighty people, with a lot of personalities from minority groups. I always wanted big classes. You can have more fun. You make a more marvelous sound. It's a more exciting thing that happens with all those voices. I'm a great, true believer in the power of the human voice. To me, that's the most marvelous tool we have. People who develop that tool develop their ego. They're going to stand in front of people and relate to them, perform. An absolute transformation comes over one student after another when they've been terribly nervous about ever letting you even hear their voice and suddenly they know that it's *there*, working well for them, and their peers are so appreciative. I mean, they give each other so much support. People come out of it really wanting *each other* to do well.

We did the All-State Honor Choir, which was quite a challenge for the kids. They could audition for it, and be selected or not. And I always did art song literature for a festival run by the Music Education Association. That was all extra work. For I can't tell you how long, I've never had any free time. I didn't go up for lunch with the teachers, and I didn't have my prep period, because it was more fun to see if I could stimulate and excite the kids. I had a sign-up sheet for solo work, training voices so they could function better. I'd take fifteen minutes for each person, but there would always be kids complaining because they didn't get a position on the list.

The amount of work was overwhelming. I worked on the weekends. I wanted to find absolutely the best material. A lot of times, I arranged most of my material myself. You can't always find exactly the right stuff for the particular group you have, so you're better off if you do your own. I was writing four-part things to be used for vocalization. I loved writing things that the kids liked the sound of, that were harmonically very beautiful. In the course of their exercises, I'd give them a musically satisfying experience.

My husband really had to take it, because I did not make myself available for him all the time. He got used to realizing that I'd be out performing on Tuesday night and maybe on Friday night, and that I'd be having kids over on Thursday night or often on the weekend. One year, for nine Saturdays in a row, I had the kids come over at nine in the morning and leave at three in the afternoon because we were doing a

special thing at the College. That's the kind of time it can
take if you want to do something special. But I don't think you can do vocal teaching otherwise. You've got to face that it's a damn commitment. You just don't stay in the business unless you give it a lot of your time. You won't have a program. If you're an English teacher, you can be a deadhead; if you're a math teacher you can be a deadhead, an unimaginative person—and you'll still have students, because they have to take your class. But you don't keep a program if you're a deadhead and you're in vocal music. You might as well just forget it. You've got to take a more aggressive approach.

These special events are what makes it so appealing for the kids. We always had things happening. We went to perform at an elegant celebration for a professional acting company, a very prestigious thing. We performed at the Mall and all over the city. They absolutely loved it, even though it took a hell of a lot of their time. We would end up making money that way, too. We performed for the Savings and Loan Association on Saturdays, or the Merchants' Association—and they'd always pay us. Particularly during the Christmas period, it was just one performance after another. Had I not made all these things happen, it wouldn't have been as jazzy a program. It makes it apparent that you're moving somewhere.

Even though the work was demanding, I think I could have stayed at that job forever. But as time went on, the purse strings were pulled tighter. We have been watching in this district the demise of one program after another after another. Curiously enough, the schools maintained the instrumental teaching, which was the expensive program and the elitist program, because it only benefitted a handful of kids. But they did away with that program which uses the instrument that each of us has: the human voice. In 1976, they eliminated vocal music from elementary schools altogether. And all the programs were dying in the middle schools. Some of our best people were let go because they were not encouraged to experiment. We had a dippy superintendent of music, an organization man slapping you on the back, and not an intelligent person at all. So several of the people who had been excellent in middle schools left and went to other areas—Santa Barbara, Boston, and so on. Then several of the people in the high school area, once the programs were killed in the elementary schools and the middle schools, just couldn't hack it anymore. It's too hard to get kids into vocal music unless they've had some early experience that attracted them to it.

I began to lose the black kids and the minority kids because they hadn't been prepared in junior high school. It was very threatening for them to come into vocal music when their voices were uncertain. I tended not to get them anymore; I tended to get just the middle-class kids who wanted to be in the musicals and be in the festivals and learn the art songs. That didn't have the same appeal for the blacks. The black kids had made an enormous difference in the success of the program. I found them so ready to learn and so interested, but I couldn't get them into my program. They began to view it as just for middle-class whites.

Frankly, I got very, very fatigued by the behavior of these flakey, middle-class kids. Very often they were quite brilliant—but bizarre. The latest aberration was that in the spring musicals we put on every year we would have no heterosexual relationships. The kids who stayed after school to work in the musical, the romantic relationships which they formed with each other were all homosexual. The young drama teacher didn't find this hard to deal with, but I did. I've always wanted to direct behavior and to feel that I was somehow elevating the kids' consciousness, but now I just felt that I was sitting idly by and watching. It wasn't necessarily a real phenomenon at all, but it was just considered jazzy to be homosexual. So these kids went this route experimentally, and we were supposed to be very compassionate when we listened to a young man saying, "Jeff really hates me and won't have anything to do with me. I simply don't know what I'm ever going to *do!*" There'd be a lot of sitting together backstage, and a great deal of touching and lying down on each other. I just began to think, "I can't take this." I felt like I was bucking the tide. I guess a lot of teachers feel like they're having to buck the tide because of the behavior of students.

Even though the program was going downhill, I maintained my commitment. I think I did as good a job as anybody, under the circumstances. In fact, I said to myself, "You must be a damn *magician* to pull this off with as little help as you're getting." To have a good program, you've got to know what you're doing and believe in it and not be discouraged by what happens. If all indications are that it's not possible to run a vocal music program, you say, "Sure, it's possible. I'll do it." It takes a lot of energy and drive and an absolute refusal to be beaten down. But when you get to the point where you've resisted that for a long time, that's when the burn-out gets massive.

I'm very definitely a pragmatist. I never have felt sorry for myself. Teaching is just something that has to be done. Some-

times it brings you satisfaction and sometimes it doesn't—
and you've got to keep it going even if it doesn't. You've got
to extract whatever joys you can out of it. And when you get
to the point where you have utterly exhausted yourself—and
I got there—then you have to call it quits. The personal cost
to yourself becomes just too great.

This past year in June I left Jefferson, and my friend Sandy,
who also ran a successful vocal music program at Jackson
High School, left for a sabbatical because she was burned
out. That was just about it. Those were the last two programs
left. For both my friend and me, the exhaustion was overwhelming: to try to run a program when you're bucking
everything.

Actually, I almost quit the year before last. In fact, this
retirement was called "the second annual Juliet Sherwood
retirement party." I got almost there, but there were a couple
of kids who were very dear to me and they were really press-
ing me to hang around. It was important for them that I stay,
and I said, "What the hell, I can probably handle one more
year." So I stayed. When I decided, it was only two or three
days before my retirement party. The retirement gift was all
initialled and everything.

A funny thing happened last year: I became "Teacher of
the Year" for the entire city. I mean, that's ridiculous: I was
at the low point of my career. I thought, "Now they're making
me the teacher of the year?" Maybe I had deserved it in the
past on a couple of occasions, but not now. I was just treading
water.

There were multiple problems that caused me to quit, but
one of the big ones was that the number of periods in the
school day were confined to six, whereas it had been eight.
That meant that the kids had fewer opportunities for electives. It was just hell getting kids into the music program. In
order to go to the State University, they had to have a certain
number of years of science and a certain number of years of
math and so on. The counselors didn't want to waste the
kids' time with things like music. Then anytime we would
perform, everybody would say, "It was so marvelous. What
you've done is so great." But in order to get there it was utter
harrassment. It was a real fight all the way.

In my later years at Jefferson I used to feel like I was pros-
tituting myself, because I would actually do anything to get
kids into the program. Nobody else was as pushy as I was.
When my numbers were small, I would go to the counselors'
office and talk to the people I knew there and tell them I was
ready and willing to take anybody, literally anybody, into

my program. I'd write letters to them explaining that a lot of the other teachers were screaming about the extra kids they had in their classes, whereas it would be a matter of *joy* for me to have them—so why not give them to me?

I became very aware that only certain things were getting extra attention in public schools. One of them is E.S.L., English as a Second Language: money pouring in, new teachers, teachers who are Oriental. At the same time they've been knocking all our own teachers who have been teaching up to thirteen years. If you haven't taught fourteen years, you're automatically fired every June. Maybe they'll bring you back, maybe they won't. I find this very hard to take.

They have a burgeoning program in special education, and a marvelous program for gifted students. But nobody gives one damn about people who aren't in any of these categories. So you have to just sit there and watch the majority of students becoming human failures. Year after year, the same number of kids come to graduate from high school with third-grade reading skills. That seems shocking to me, and evil. They never do one damn thing about it in elementary school; they never give the elementary school teachers the assistance they need. That's where they need to learn how to read, not in high school. I find the inadequacy of our educational system more than I can handle. It's a very dismaying, frustrating, painful thing for me. I have a sense of desperation about the school system. I just don't think we're going in the right direction.

I try not to let this affect me too personally. I'm sixty-two years old. People might think that I've retired, but I haven't. I'm getting involved in a program now to try to bring music back into the public elementary schools, where it's totally disappeared for years. We're establishing a class at the Conservatory—for up to thirty fourth- and fifth-grade teachers. We'll pay them ten dollars for each time that they come, and give the schools that are able to form music programs as a result of this course five hundred dollars. We're trying to get foundation money to do it.

I'm also teaching a class in vocal music at Adams Junior High School, just two mornings a week. I don't want to do it unless they pay me. I don't want to become anybody's sucker; I don't think that's a good thing for the rest of the teaching profession. So they're paying me at Adams, and they'll be paying me for my teachers' class at the Conservatory. I'd like to do the part-time teaching at a couple of other schools, but they have to figure out a way to raise the money. I have a school that wants to take me on as a full-time person, but I don't want to do that at this point in my life. I'd rather go to a lot of different schools and just do a little bit here and a little bit there. I'd like to feel that a whole bunch of children were having access to a singing experience. I want so very much to have kids get to sing. It's terrible that they don't. They're so open and responsive to it.

The *last* thing I would do is send a resumé to the private schools, because I don't really believe in private education. But I may end up doing that if I can't get enough to do otherwise—just so I'd have the pleasure of continuing to reach out for people to teach vocal music, without having to get caught in that damn treadmill that you're in if you're in a particular school, and only that school. I still love to teach, but I want to do it under circumstances that are pleasurable.

I want to find out what else I'm capable of doing, too. I don't want to be confined to the same old track. I feel the need to be liberated, to not be busy around the clock. For as long as I can remember, I never had any time to myself. It was like being on an escalator. You go up, and then you come down on the other side, then up again, then down again. That's what it's like to be teaching school. I feel that I have to get away from it. I'd love to do something that's exciting and different and unusual as far as my thought processes. I have to get to a point in my life where I'm able to be in my house and find out what is here and find out what my needs are and make some of the friends that I've wanted to make but haven't had the time to develop. So far, I must say I've enjoyed it thoroughly.

Commentary

W hat do these stories have in common? I see two sig- nificant threads running through the self-portraits you have just read: the teachers are extremely dedicated to their ideals and to the children, yet they often seem to be trapped by a feeling of personal helplessness in the face of the jobs that are expected of them. They talk about how much they love their work, and almost in the same breath they go on to complain about the incessant pressures of the school en- vironment: heavy workloads, overcrowded classes, excessive paperwork, administrative intrusions, budgetary cutbacks. In addition to these institutional problems, the teachers talk about the personal problems created by their jobs: losing sight of ideals amid day-to-day realities, trying in vain to live up to their own unrealistic expectations, neglecting their families, working themselves to a point of frenzy yet still feeling guilty for never doing enough. And they talk, too, of the social demands endemic to the teaching profession: the unrelenting frequency of personal interactions, the need to enforce discipline, the need to maintain self-control, the need to motivate students with diverse interests, the need to sat- isfy the conflicting expectations of administrators, parents, and children.

All these problems are cumulative, feeding upon each other and multiplying through time. As the years creep by, they tend to create a negative assessment of one's work—and of one's sense of self-worth. Ideals which once reigned supreme become harder to maintain. The teachers begin to tire; de- spite their dedication, sincerity, and empathy for the stu- dents, there comes a time when many of them are tempted to give it all up. Their cumulative discontent, sometimes bordering on paranoia or despair, seems to call out for some sort of assertive action. They feel they have to do something to take control of their professional well-being.

And so it is that many teachers, after putting in their first few years of inspired service, begin to play the Quitting Game. Rae Johnson, Steve Adams, David Reynolds, Frances Marinara, Helen McKenna, Juliet Sherwood—they have all played the game, and some are still playing it. The Quitting Game goes something like this: each year a teacher tells himself, quite sincerely, "This is my last year of teaching." Generally, the prediction does not come true: come September the teachers once again will be in the classroom, ready for one more last year in school, and ready to play yet another round of the Quitting Game. In the words of Helen McKenna, "I've been playing this game for the past ten years, but I haven't recognized it as a game yet. Each time I tell myself that this is my last year, I really mean it."

Why do teachers insist on continually deluding themselves? What do they get from such ritualistic antics?

The Quitting Game gives us teachers an illusory sense of renewal. It is our own silly way of recapturing our destiny, of confronting our powerlessness, of taking charge of our lives. It enables us to tackle our jobs one year at a time, since anything longer than that would appear too oppressive. It is a trick we use for our personal rejuvenation. There are other tricks, too, which are not quite so devious. The more tricks, the better. In one way or another, teachers have to devise ways of coping with the passage of time in their professional careers.

Time constitutes a critical dimension of any work experience. Time and rhythm. Rhythm gives texture to the vast expanse of time. People break time apart in order to imbue it with meaning. God gives us some natural rhythms—days, lunar months, years—but that is not enough. In order to get on with our business, we find it helpful to fabricate others: weeks, quarters, semesters, and forty-five minute periods for math or English, with five minutes for passing or fifteen minutes for recess. Untamed, time seems to do us no good: we only get older and die. Harnessed into rhythmic cycles, it facilitates our social organization and helps us cope with life's tedious toils.

Teachers tend to understand time and rhythm better than most other workers. We have to. We know that children are fresh and alert in the morning, sleepy after lunch, restless toward the end of the day—and we schedule our activities accordingly. The days of the week, too, take on unique characteristics which help distinguish between appropriate and inappropriate activities. Our sensitivity to the children's natural rhythms can lead to a better appreciation of our own: the attitude we bring to work on Monday or Tuesday is not necessarily the same as our attitude on Thursday or Friday.

Each year in the classroom has a familiar sense of rhythm. In September we start fresh: new children, new ideas, new input. Through the early fall we are propelled by this newness, and by the energy we have stored over the summer. As excitement slowly drifts back to routine, we hit our steady stride. The tenor and complexion of our class is established. We start plugging away; we cover ground. As routine drifts farther backwards into boredom, we cast our eyes forward to the winter holidays.

Come January, we know we're in for the long haul. We find our stride once again, but by February or March we have to reach deep into our bag of tricks to keep ourselves awake at the wheel. The weather breaks, Easter comes and goes, and the end of the year is in sight. The knowledge that relief is just around the corner allows us to turn on the steam, to give it one last burst of energy before we finally collapse.

The daily rhythms, the seasonal rhythms, we can handle. But what about the larger picture: the years, the decades? Where is the basic rhythm, the texture, of our professional careers?

The teaching profession, as it is traditionally construed, is "flat." It deals inadequately with the developmental processes of adulthood, with aging, with the passage of time in a person's life. There is no sense of movement, no distinction between apprentice, journeyman, and master craftsman. A teacher is simply a teacher, whether it's his fourth year or his fortieth. His work profile, his responsibilities, remain virtually unchanged over time.

Yet change is endemic to our modern world. Our society is constantly on the go, avoiding stagnation like the plague. We hype ourselves up with "new and improved" gimmicks to capture our imagination and appeal to our fancy. This leads to a dangerous source of conflict: the outside culture is fluid, while our work appears static. Our schools do not provide adequate outlets for the variation and mobility encouraged by the rest of our culture.

Forty years, in a restless world, is a long time to stay at the same job, a job that permits no significant changes. Not many teachers today can enter the classroom in their twenties and still be happy and fulfilled in their work when they retire at sixty-five. Let's take a retrospective look, for instance, at the teachers whom we have met in these pages:

Sarah Rosen, at the outset of her career, cannot even begin to conceive of such a time span. It boggles her imagination, and it seems to frighten her.

Lynda Kime, with all her enthusiasm, might be able to handle it. But at the age of twenty-five, her enthusiasm has yet to withstand the test of time: she still has thirty-nine and a half years to go.

Rae Johnson, after only five years, demonstrates definite signs of fatigue. The job is wearing her down; already, she appears ready for a change.

Sage Looney left the classroom before turning thirty. For her, another thirty-five years, facing eight hundred students each year, would be unthinkable.

Steve Adams, after fifteen years, wants "to get out while the getting's good." He craves a world of possibilities which are denied him within the classroom.

David Reynolds, in the interests of keeping the dandruff off his jacket, has already bailed out once. He is now back on the job and seemingly contented, at least for the time being. But his renewed energy stems directly from a dramatic change in his personal life.

Frances Marinara is upset. A change seems overdue. She is not particularly ambitious in the worldly sense, but she is tired of suffering humiliation. As an ordinary classroom teacher, she resents being stuck at the bottom of a pecking order she does not believe in.

Helen McKenna, after twenty years, is halfway there. But she has had enough. Admittedly ambitious, she is moving into administration—and therefore out of the classroom—to broaden her horizons.

Annie Waugh, more than any of the other teachers, seems happy to remain in the classroom indefinitely. But she too felt forced to move from job to job until she finally settled into a situation which suited her.

Juliet Sherwood has a natural bent for working with youngsters, but time has taken its toll. Unable to adjust to the institutional limitations being imposed upon her, she feels forced to look for new work—even as she approaches the age of retirement.

It seems that most of these teachers are struggling—sometimes graciously, sometimes desperately—with the relationship between time and work. This is what the Quitting Game is all about, and this is why so many teachers, although apparently fulfilled by the obvious meaning in their work, begin to look beyond the classroom for the satisfaction of their professional aspirations.

Chapter Two
Beyond
the Classroom—
and Back

Hungry for change, but denied meaningful change within the flatness of a normal career, teachers are tempted in various directions: they can bail out, exploring new fields outside of education; they can look for new teaching jobs in other institutions, hoping somehow that the new jobs will differ from the old ones; they can "climb the ladder" into administration, the apparent (though often illusory) locus of power in the schools. If they choose to stay within the educational field, many teachers will do whatever they can to salvage some sense of personal fluidity in a basically static profession.

elementary and high school # William
principal, two weeks before
retirement # Nicholas

When I came out of the Service, I went right into teaching
at the junior high school level. First it was science, then I
moved from that into physical education and a core curriculum of English and social studies with delinquent-type children—not really "delinquent," but kids with problems in
school. At the same time I was working on my master's and
also on my administrative credential, because I knew I wanted
to go into administration. I liked teaching very much, I enjoyed my classrooms extremely well—but I knew I wanted
to climb. I've always led myself up to supervisory positions.
Anything I ever did, I always was a climber. That's just the
nature of the beast in me.

Anyway, I got married and my wife and I were teaching
at the same school. That's not permitted in Los Angeles, so
I had to make a switch to another school. I spent four years
in the Los Angeles school system. Then my wife and I got a
divorce. I went up to Yosemite and got into the resort management business for the next eight years. So I was totally
out of education.

I left Yosemite because of a change in the management
situation up there. I had already reached as far as I was going
to go in the company; I saw I wasn't going to go any farther.
I wasn't sure what I was going to do then. I explored various
fields, possibly going into the ski resort or hotel business. I
ended up with a job offer from the Job Corps, a War on
Poverty program, in the Bay Area. So I went to work there
for two years as an instructor, the two most fantastic years I
ever had in my life. I really enjoyed it. These were real problem kids, kids from off the streets of New York, New Jersey.
I loved going to work, loved the whole job. I relate better
with problem kids than I do academic kids. I have more of
a personal interest in them, an empathy toward them. And
I feel they need help. It's two things: I get something from

them, and they get something from me. I get the satisfaction
of helping someone.

I was there for two years, and then the Job Corps program
was folding up. I had a chance to go to the east side of the
Sierras as a principal: a small, comprehensive high school
serving about two hundred and thirty students. That was my
first administrative job at the educational level. I was about
forty years old at the time. I was there for four years, and
then the district was going through a change. They had ousted
two superintendents; there was a major change in the district
board. The superintendent's job is a very political job. A high
school principal is political too, but not nearly like a superintendent's job. At the plant level, you're still dealing with
kids. You're still more engrossed with that than you are with
the politics of what's going on around you in the community.
Frequently, the superintendent will use a principal as his
grinding ax. A head hunter. He's got to chop somebody because of what's happening in the community. He'll put the
pressure on whomever he can at the lower level to save
himself. I think that was going on; I felt it was going on. I
thought, "Better get out of here." Which I did: I left there. I
did not have a job to go to at that point.

I left there and moved up to a place in the Sierras. Soon I
got a job as a vice-principal down in the Valley. It was a
large school, seven hundred fifty students, and it was a
chaotic mess. There was no discipline in the school. The
superintendent thought I was the best thing that ever hit
that school, because I started structuring things, setting it up.
The faculty thought I was fantastic. But I hated the job, because it was nothing but discipline. I had all the functions
to go to: the athletic functions, and all the dances. I had to
watch for the discipline, watch for the problems—and there
were a lot of them. There were fights; there were drugs. It
was heavy into everything, every kind of problem you can
imagine. Students bulldozing and knocking houses down,
running into downtown with bulldozers and hitting buildings. It was a disaster when I arrived there. Well, within
about a year, a little over a year, I had the thing cleaned up.
We didn't have the same discipline problems. I used con-
sistency, and calling people on the carpet right then and
there when it happened. Calling the parents, and getting
the parents involved. The teachers backed me a hundred
percent, because for the first time they had a chance to have
somebody who was going to do something to see that the
kids got punished.

I definitely got some satisfaction out of trying to clean that place up. I was helping the system, so teachers would have more time to do the job that they're in there for, without being bothered with these discipline problems they had. But I wasn't happy with my life at that point, because everything I was doing seemed negative to me. I wasn't building anything that looked *great* to me. It was helping the teachers, it was helping the school—but it wasn't doing anything for me. I wanted to get out of there as soon as I could. I mean, sometimes I just hated going to work.

I had a chance to come up here to Kenny. I've been here eight years, which has been too long. I loved my job when I first came up here. I loved coming to work every day. I was totally involved in every aspect that I could. I attended everything there was. A twelve-hour, eighteen-hour day was nothing. Working weekends, nothing.

Again, this place had serious problems when I arrived, and that's one of the reasons the board picked me. They had already checked on my past history, and they thought I was the man for cleaning up the school. When I arrived here, it was all on independent study. There was no structure. The faculty was demoralized. (They are demoralized now, too, but that's another story.) The place was in shambles. The office was total chaos. You'd never know somebody with any management skills had ever been in there.

So there was a lot for me to do here, and that was exciting. There were some personnel that had to be moved out in one way or another. You don't fire personnel; you put pressure on them. You try to help them look for another job. If a person isn't happy, they're probably looking anyway. You just help them along, and you needle them a little. Usually they're inefficient, and you pressure them in these areas where they're weak. You report on them. Sure, you also make an effort to help them improve, to show them why they are doing things wrong. If they're already that far gone, though, there isn't much chance for them to make improvement. I have one man here now that no matter what I've done, I haven't been able to make a dent in him. All the principals that have been here before, they weren't able to either. He shouldn't be in the teaching field. He knows he shouldn't be in here too, but he's getting ready to retire and the only reason he's here is for the bucks.

I'd have to say that for the last two years I've been here, probably the same thing is true for me: I shouldn't be here. It's a combination of various things: my own lifestyle, the students, the parents. The students aren't getting properly trained at home. They know that we have no real control over them here at school. We can't do anything to them. I'm not talking about physical violence; I've never been one to hit a student. But you should be able to discuss it with the student and call the parent in if need be, and then the parent puts the pressure on the kid. Well, I don't find that happening anymore.

The caliber of teachers, too: I find they are somewhat permissive themselves. They're not as structured. I get irritated with them because I still believe in rules and regulations, and I find that the teachers cannot accept these. They're very loose, and these things are getting to me.

A couple of years ago, I started looking for other jobs elsewhere. Three places, I made it to the interview stage, but I never got the job. To be called for an interview is pretty good these days, because there are sometimes six or seven hundred people applying for one job, and less than half a dozen will make it to that stage. To get that close means that your papers are in pretty good shape. But I'm not articulate. When it comes to the final interview, this is not one of my strengths. I don't make the grade. Last year I was called for an interview down in the Santa Cruz area, but I did not even bother to go to it. I figured, "I've only got two more years till I'm fifty-five. I'll cash in and get the hell out. Then maybe I'll do something else."

So the last two years, I've just done my job. I should have left. I don't feel good about that. I don't think any man can feel good about himself if he stays on a job he doesn't like and isn't giving it his all—and I have not given my all to this job the last two years. If a man is going to feel good about himself, he needs to feel like he's accomplishing something. He has to be doing more than just the routine, satisfactory job of running a school from point A to point B. Anybody can do that. I'm doing that now. I'm not going to leave this place in a shambles, but I'm not putting in anything creative or constructive.

I told myself a year ago that this would be my last year here and I would put my wholehearted effort into it and really get back like I was years ago. It didn't happen. I don't know whether it was me, not having the ability to do it anymore, or. . . . I don't like my faculty very much. I think it's mutual: they don't like me. I'm not a warm person. I can be warm to students, but I cannot be warm to adults as well. I've never associated with my faculty. I've never gone out with them, partied with them. I don't go to their houses; I don't have any of them at my house. I've always been somewhat like that. I'm pretty much of a loner. I've always kept my distance from the people I work around. I find it works effectively for me. At times it can be somewhat lonely, but I operate better that way. I'm more comfortable that way.

I don't share many interests with my faculty. I'm not very involved in the subjects they teach. I am not a strong curriculum person. I'm stronger in management and control and supervising. I'm not saying that that's what a principal *should* be; I think he should be a well-balanced individual. My strengths are in detail, accounting, books, setting up things—particularly going into an area that has had problems and straightening the school up. I clean house: put the paperwork in order, get rid of some problem teachers. This has happened to me frequently: I go into an area; I put a lot of energy into it; I get things in shape, and then after about four years I have a tendency to get bored. I want something new. I want something to grab onto again, to go for. I don't know how some of these people do it: when I was growing up, some of these people were in administration forever. But then again, I saw that they didn't do anything except maintain. There was nothing new that was happening in the schools.

The job of an administrator has become a lot more complicated over the past twenty years. The schools have been going through such turmoil and changes. Everybody's gotten into the school act; everybody thinks they have a panacea for making it better. It's constantly changing, changing, changing. Administrators can't keep up with all the things that are going on anymore. It used to be that all you had to worry about was the curriculum and the kids in the school. Today, you have the S.I.P. [School Improvement Program] to worry about, you've got the vocational ed. programs, you've got all the parental committees coming in—which I think are beneficial, but it certainly puts a lot more pressure on the administrator. You've got all the special programs, and they all have carrots hanging on the end of a stick. They've got the money dangling out front, so you've got to go for that carrot because the money is there. Supposedly that's to improve the quality of education, but you're going off in fifteen different directions trying to reach all these carrots. You're going for the buck, and you're going for anything that will get it for you. You've got to get more money for your school, because the purse strings are being closed up on the state level and the county level. It's very trying on the administrator. All these programs require committees; reporting, paperwork. A lot of the work is wasted. I'm sure that a lot of these reports we have to fill out are not read by anybody but just piled up in some cubicle. But you have to justify that money that you got; you've got to be accountable for it in some way.

In most schools, the principal is too busy with the routine of the office, submerged behind his desk. Most of us, including myself, spend too much time doing detail work, discipline work, paper work. We always call it essential, although a lot of times you could get by without it—find somebody else to do it, delegate it. I spend too much time in my office, no question about it. I should be out more in the yard, out around the students, and in the classroom helping the teachers—not so much from the observation point of what they're doing wrong, but suggesting some better ways of doing things. But like I say, I'm better at details. I'm not a warm personality. When I go to a faculty meeting, I've got it all laid out: "Bing, bing, bing." But I'm not sure all these "bing, bing, bing" things I have written down are really important. I may be well-organized at these faculty meetings, but it may be a big waste of time. My time might be better spent helping them with their teaching. I used to do more of that. That's a measure of how I've sluffed off in my job.

Another measure is I'm not going to the extracurricular activities that I used to go to. I used to go to everything that anybody put on; I was always there to give them my support. Sometimes I still go, but my support is half-hearted because I don't really want to be there. I try not to show it, but it probably radiates to some degree. I keep hoping it doesn't, but I can't believe that it doesn't.

They had a square dance here the other day for the fifth and sixth grades. Six o'clock. I like to be home watching my news at six o'clock, having a martini. Couldn't do that. Came out to the square dance; watched the square dance; went up to the participants afterwards and told each one of them how good they did. I did everything I knew I was supposed to do, but I didn't want to be there at all. I wanted to be home in my comfortable chair, in my own house, having a martini watching the news.

I still want things to function. I still want to have a school when I leave here that's not going downhill too badly. I know I'm going downhill, but I don't want anybody else to know. I'm sure they know it anyway. I don't like myself very much right now as an administrator—haven't for the last two years. Two years ago, if I knew it would turn out like this . . . well, I might have stayed with it anyway. Knowing that the retirement money would be there, I'd probably do exactly what I did. I wish I could say I wouldn't, but I probably would.

I don't know what I'm going to do when I leave this job.

I could become an alcoholic very easily. I have been one; I am one now. I keep it under control by putting barriers up in front of myself. I do not allow myself to drink until I leave the job. I do not allow myself to drink when there's an activity at school at night. That's why I hate extracurricular activities, because I can't drink until I get home. I do not like weekend events, because I cannot drink all during the weekend. But I have to put those barriers up, or I would not be able to survive on the job.

Without my job, there will be no barriers. That's a big question mark for me. I've got to find some other barriers, like maybe another job, or being very strongly disciplined with myself. On a Saturday or Sunday when I don't have anything to do, I say five o'clock is martini time. I don't allow myself to do any drinking before that so I can accomplish some work. I've found in recent years, though, that that doesn't hold out. Sometimes I'll break down and have a drink earlier.

I don't have a family; I'm not hurting anybody except myself. I drink every day—I've drunk every day in my life for thirty or forty years, or whatever it is. There's no question I'm an alcoholic, I know that. Anybody who needs it that much is an alcoholic. It has interfered a few times in my life with my job: twice up on the east side of the Sierras when I did not come to work on a Monday morning; another time when I had a few drinks, which I shouldn't have, and went to a parents' night at school. I had to get up in front of an audience. From what I gather, it turned out to be sort of funny. They didn't know I was drinking; they just thought I was amusing. But it has not interfered here at Kenny, because I keep my self-discipline during the week and I go to bed very early on Sunday, like seven o'clock. I get up on Monday and I'm ready to go.

What happens when I leave here, I don't know. If I see I cannot handle it anymore by self-discipline, then I may have to do something about it. But I feel I've survived so far, and I enjoy my drinking. I'm happy when I have my drink. Things are a lot better, so that's why I do it. I know very well from other people that there's a better way, but I don't know how to get there right now.

Bill Honig

newly elected State Superintendent of Schools, two weeks before taking office

I came into teaching in an unusual way. I started out as an attorney. I graduated from Boalt Law School, clerked for the Supreme Court, and then went to work in state government for Governor Pat Brown, Sr. Since I did developmental work for education policy at the state level, my introduction to the field came from the top.

I then joined a private law firm in San Francisco and became involved in the Constitutional Rights Foundation, a program where lawyers teach junior high and high school students about law. I got in the classroom, and realized how fulfilling that was. Teaching was what I wanted to do, so I left law. I worked for a couple of years with the Model Cities Program, developing community education programs around the nation. Then I said: "Look, I've seen education all over from the top, but I've never really taught." So I joined the Teacher Corps and received my Master's in Teaching at San Francisco State College.

I taught for four and a half years at Luther Burbank Elementary School. I taught an E.H. [Educationally Handicapped] class for my first half-year, then a fifth grade, then a combination fourth, fifth, and sixth grade. I was tired at the end of that period. Elementary teaching is draining to me because of the continual emotional transactions. If you're going to be there for the children, you're always giving something emotionally.

I had never been trained for my work with the E.H. class and I had to figure out my own way that first half-year. There were some really rough kids in the class. I was relatively isolated; the administration didn't give me any help. But nobody can really do it for you. You've got to learn things that become second nature the second or third year of teaching. The first year you're very vulnerable, and the students are smart enough to pick that up. It took me two or three

months just to get things calmed down to the point where
the children were learning. Then I felt pretty good; the class
was under control. But the emotional trauma you go through
while this is happening . . . you're thrown back on your own
emotional resilience. Teaching is a pretty isolated profession.

When I taught at Second Community [an alternative public
school], the faculty did talk a lot. That was the whole theory
of the school. There was a lot of joint planning. That worked
well, at least by the third year. The first year it was a new
school, and nobody was clear about objectives. There was a
conflict between the students being told, "It's a free school,
you can do anything you want," and those of us who were
saying, "That's not what we're trying to do here." The second
year, there was a lot of tension between different groups of
parents. It blew up a couple of times. Finally we got that
settled. The third year was terrific. The school was under
control, and everybody really liked what they were doing.
The children loved it; they felt a part of it. The atmosphere
was great. All the work payed off. The students' test results
for math and reading were at the top for San Francisco public
schools.

During my last year of teaching, Governor Jerry Brown
appointed me to the State Board of Education. I was the first
teacher on the Board, so I found myself back into formulating
policy at the top. I had the role in the classroom and the role
in a fairly prestigious position right in the center of policy.
I decided: "This is going to be my career. I'm going to try to
make an impact in the public schools."

After I finished teaching, I was very interested in staff
development: teacher training, how you upgrade teachers'
skills, and so forth. I wrote my own project and received
funding from the San Francisco Foundation. I worked with
board members, principals, and superintendents, and I wrote
a manual on reading, which is still widely used.

After being in this staff development project, it was clear
to me that one of the major problems in education is the way
it's run. The superintendents, the principals and the boards
really had been neglecting the product. What's taught, how
it's taught, the support level, the incentive systems—that's
what makes the difference in good districts. So I tried to
organize a group of superintendents, the best superintendents in the state, who were curriculum-oriented, who ran
good districts and had good results. I just was starting to get
that group together when the people at the State Department
of Education became afraid of our efforts and began sabo-
taging them.

I had the same feeling as I had had about teaching: if you're going to talk about something, you should have done it. So I decided, "Look, I'm interested in administration. It's something that's exciting, so I'm going to get a job *doing* it." It was somewhat of a long shot; I didn't have any administrative experience. I took the administrative test, which was not a good test. There were four or five central, driving ideas that the publishers wanted to get across. They had certain stock principles. I had been working in staff development, so I knew the subject. They asked a lot of questions about staff development. I knew what they wanted me to answer, but these answers were dead wrong. I intentionally answered about one-third of the questions incorrectly. I answered the way they wanted and reached the ninety-ninth percentile on the exam. That tells you something about the test.

Anyway, I received the credential. The first job I applied for was in Piedmont, and I didn't even make the first cut for an interview. Then a woman I knew called me up about three months later and said, "Do you know anybody who would be interested in being a superintendent?" I said, "Yes, me." So I applied, and I was selected out of a hundred and twenty people.

It was absolutely fortuitous. There were three new school board members who had just run on the platform of high expectations, core curriculum, and high standards—all the things I've been saying in my campaign. They took a risk with me, because they liked my philosophy and my background. We turned that district around in about two years. I had good rapport with the teachers. They saw it was to their advantage to beef up the program, because they were losing their jobs. They were losing kids to private schools, which had a thousand children on their waiting lists. The public schools weren't teaching science; they weren't teaching history in a comprehensive manner. They didn't have the respect of the children. They had problems with assemblies. The kids were very rude, but nobody did anything. The district had administrative problems; personnel needed to be changed. We put in two good principals, and basically revamped the district. We added courses and extended the school day. It worked—our efforts really paid off. The scores went up; the attitudes of our staff improved. That was a very satisfying experience.

In my experience, things are always forced upon you before you're really ready. Two years into that job, when it was just starting to click really well, I became involved in a philosophical battle with the Riles administration [Wilson Riles,

Honig's predecessor as California State Superintendent of Public Instruction] over the issue of: "Our children aren't taking enough science, math and English. The program is too permissive, in the sense of not demanding enough. We're trying to accommodate the students by lowering the expectation level. The system is just not performing well enough, and we're going to lose it if we don't turn it around." Originally it looked like Riles' administration was going to buy that philosophy. I wrote a speech for Riles saying how the state should set broader standards for what the students should be taking. Unfortunately, he didn't deliver the speech.

I was still serving on the State Board during that time. We held a year's worth of hearings in 1980 about how the students were not taking the right courses, the low homework levels, and the discipline problems.

At that time, the philosophy in many of the districts was: "The child should be making a lot of the choices." The idea of a reading list was anathema to a lot of people. I said, "Wait a minute. That's our culture. The repository of our heritage is found in books, found in our history, found in biography. We, as adults, have a responsibility to put children in contact with that. We have to convince people of what's ideal. That's what a curriculum should be: an adult choice. You can't teach everything, so you choose what kinds of experiences are elevating." That was a different point of view than had been prevalent for the past ten years. The idea of telling a child that he should read a certain book was going against the grain. So it was a philosophical argument between a student-driven instructional program—a lot of electives, a lot of accommodation for children who weren't making it— and one that says, "Let's set the standards high and help them do it."

We weren't giving the kids enough homework. Homework, to me, is such an easy way of extending the class hours. If a child is in class five or six hours a day and he does an hour of homework a night, you've got about seventeen percent more time that he's working. It's a powerful teaching tool, one we shouldn't throw away. But the homework levels of the state were really low. And the courses: if you take a look at the statistics, the students were not taking enough science or math compared to the other states. So there were some basic things that were wrong.

I wrote an article which made all these same arguments I'm making now. There was no comment. I didn't hear anything. That's when it dawned on me, "You have no clout as a board member. Nobody is going to listen to you. You're just one of ten people and they all have different opinions, so why should anyone listen to you? The only way you're going to get this system turned around is to run for State Superintendent." And I convinced myself we could turn it around. I talked to enough people in the districts who were doing the same thing I was, so there was no question it could be done. It wasn't something that was just a dream.

What actually happened is that I got angry. To me it was clear what needed to be done. Every time I'd state my point of view most educators would say, "That's an elitist position, a racist position. You're pandering to the right wing." People tend to see things in stark political terms: "If you're for homework or discipline, you're a right-winger. If you believe students can learn, you're a right-winger." My philosophy was out of vogue, and my major goal was to make it legitimate. My campaign for State Superintendent of Public Instruction was to educate the leadership in the state and the general public that: "This is a legitimate point of view, and it's the way we've got to go in California." By the results of the election, my ideas were validated. That's what people want.

The first battle has been won. Now the question is getting people to do something about it. That's why the superintendent's position is so important. I'm a salesman for this point of view, trying to find allies in the field—teachers, principals, and board members—who want to cooperate and implement the kind of program that will truly educate our children.

There's something that happens in the workshops we give that has to do with renewal. Teachers rarely get to come together with teachers within their own district, let alone with teachers from all over. The fact that they're meeting people from all over the state, from other places, is fascinating to them. You can almost feel the energy created by that. The other thing that happens is that we often have teachers and administrators in on the same basic training session. They're both learning this stuff together, and that's interesting. It's a sense of newness, a breather, a refresher.

Most teachers are very isolated. Many of them don't even interact with other teachers at the same school. We'll go to schools where somebody will say, "Oh, her. She's in her room. She never comes out. She never has lunch with us." Or, "We don't see each other socially. No, we never do anything together." I kind of picture them as closed—unless they're going to school. When they're working on units or degrees, they're rubbing off on other people, and they're reading the research. That's a form of renewal also.

The workshop I did this week brought together people from a rather large city. Some of them had worked in the district for twenty years and didn't even know each other. So the workshop pulled them together, and that was wonderful for them. Lots of it was professional. I noticed they didn't really get off on outside interests. It was a lot of shop talk, a lot of sharing.

In a small district, often people don't get together there, either. People are "small" in terms of hanging onto their stuff, or wanting their little corner of the world to be better than someone else's little corner of the world. So our workshop brings them together and fosters that good stuff that comes from really being colleagues, sharing and working on problems together. You know, the old silly saying that two heads are better than one. That's always true. People foster growth when they work together. Change occurs.

Personally, I was ready for a change when I got involved in these workshops. I had become involved in a staff development group that meets in our district, with each administrator bringing one teacher from his site. I had become involved in that with my principal, and it opened my blinders. It gave me a new look at the world. It said, "Good grief, there's something out there, beyond my little classroom and my school." I began to hear new things. I began to meet new people, administrators as well as teachers.

I really began to feel the need to grow. What I had always thought was that I would quit teaching when I had everything the way I wanted it. That was an immature idea. I finally came to the realization, slowly, that that would never happen. A good teacher *never* reaches that point. Well, when that hit me, I felt, "I want to try something else."

The other alternative was administration. I took the administrative exam and passed it. Without any coursework I had my administrative credential. Then I decided administration wasn't really what I wanted. It was much too political. So this opening came up on the staff development team, and that was just right. It was still working with people, but it had no political ramifications. It's a wonderful job in that respect. I can walk into a large district, talk to the superintendent, lay it out in terms of what they need to think about and how they can make it work—and if they like it, fine, if they don't, I leave. I have nothing to gain or nothing to lose.

If I didn't get this particular job change, I had already made up my mind that I needed to go to either junior high school or kindergarten. I *needed* change. I couldn't just stay in grades four, five, or six. It got to be real "ho-hum." Not in terms of kids, but I got tired of looking at new curriculum, thinking of a new way to do it. I don't know. I just needed a personal change after fifteen years, and there weren't many choices. I could change grade levels, I could change schools—that's a change for some people. Change could be moving out of a room that they might have occupied for twenty years. I personally feel we should require teachers to make a change every fifth year, or something like that. Change schools, change grade levels, your choice. It's frightening, and that's why people resist doing it, but it's also stimulating. You work with other people.

Workshops like ours make you think more about what you're doing. Once you start thinking this way, it's hard to go on doing the same old thing. You start looking at yourself, and you foster your own change. But sometimes there's nowhere to go with that change. That's a real frustration in our schools. Fortunately, a small change can sometimes be enough for renewal. It doesn't have to be a monumental change. There are lots of ways to foster growth without changing schools or going into administration. For example, we encourage teachers to begin to do peer observations and give each other feedback. We encourage them to tape lessons. Or some teachers can become experts on interesting topics, like sexual stereotyping, and then they can spread their expertise, put on workshops. That's a way for them to grow. The problem is I don't think many districts are investigating all of those different ways to make teachers feel elevated, important, like they have a way to grow without getting out of the classroom. But there are ways to do that. If you sat around with ten people and brainstormed, you'd come up with a list of a hundred ways to encourage teacher growth, all staying within the classroom: serving on committees, being a liason between the PTA and the staff, a mini-workshop for the staff, including them in administrative chores, like writing the bulletin.

Administrators can be a part of all this. We encourage principals to teach, and allow teachers to critique them. Principals need to take risks to gain their teachers' trust. If they are going to ask their teachers to risk, they need to risk. In some districts, the superintendent has gone into every single school in his district and taught a lesson, not always with a great deal of success. Sometimes he'll fall flat on his face, but he'll allow the teachers to share with him and give him feedback. That does something for the teachers: "Here's this person who heads up the whole farm and he's taking the biggest risk of all, so I ought to be able to take just a little one."

Before I actually left the classroom, I was involved in a lot of these other types of things. I was asked to serve on several district committees. I was asked by a professor at the university to come and share some of my information with student teachers. Well, that was a real thrill! I also was involved in this ongoing staff development between teachers and principals. There were all kinds of things going on there: I learned the clinical supervision process; we worked on problem-solving models; we worked on decision-making processes; we looked at management skills and leadership techniques; we did a lot of self-analysis stuff. On the personal level, all this made me realize that even if I stayed in teaching for fifty years, I would never get to the point that originally I thought I would get to: the "perfect" teaching style. Also, it made me say, "I've done this, and I did a good job of teaching. I feel real positive about what I've done, and now I'd like to try something else."

All these committees and stuff, it was working with adults. I felt I had some particular skills personally that would make me an effective person to work with adults. But I had some problems actually leaving the classroom. I felt some real guilt. I had made some inroads into the community, and the community gave me lots of pats on the back and made me feel as though I would really be missed. So there was all this guilt: walking out on kids. But I had to say "No" to these people. I felt I could influence a whole lot more, and still be in touch with kids. I just knew in my heart that I needed to get on with something else.

It felt sometimes like I *was* walking out on kids. Particularly when you teach in the same neighborhood for a while, you've got brothers and sisters who can't wait to be in your room. Parents would just be astounded that I wasn't going to be there for their next child who was now ready for my classroom. But there will be some other good teacher who is going to be there to take my place. I think our district has good hiring policies, and so for the most part we have good people there. Some new, young, wonderful person is going to take the job, and they'll learn to love that person too.

It's kind of like the life and death process, but it's an exciting one rather than: "I can't wait till that teacher retires, because she's really not a good teacher." If you look at people changing and wanting to leave the classroom—maybe they'll go sell Avon, for all I know—that's okay. We will go out and hire new people to bring life again to the district.

I definitely feel rejuvenated by my career change. I'm even looking now at another step. I've been doing this three years, and I'm getting real irritated in terms of some of the principals that I'm working with. It's beginning to bother me that I go to a site and watch a teacher that has real potential, a really interesting person that wants to grow, and the principal does nothing with it. I leave feeling terribly frustrated. Finally, I'm coming to realize that the next logical step is to try it myself and see if I could make it work. So that's what I'm looking at now: being a principal.

I never thought I would want to do that. I didn't want the political aspect, and I still don't know how that's going to work for me personally. But I think I have some good qualities in terms of principaling. I can see now that I need to do that. It's a process of growth again.

There's no end to this; that's the exciting part. I hope the process will always lead me to something new. Whether it's within the same job description or not does not really matter. I look at it, not in terms of power or politics, but just as another job and a natural kind of progression for myself, in terms of where I've been and wherever I'm going. Who knows where that might be?

I'm always one that says, "What's the worst thing that can happen?" I can hate it, or I'll be so poor at the political end of it that I'll need to get out of it and do something else. Then I'll just follow that process. It may lead me backward, or it may lead me forward. But really, even backward is forward. In general, growth and change and renewal and all of that should always be going on, or people lose the joy in their work. That's really, in many cases, what has happened. Work has become a drudgery. You know, "Thank God it's Friday." People do anything to avoid it, instead of work being a joy, being a part of whatever is important in life. For me, work is a joy. That's the kind of person I am. I tend to be real positive, looking on the good side of things. So you need to temper what I say by that aspect of my personality.

I was like that in the classroom. I loved teaching; I loved kids. Even when I was ready for a change, work was still a joy. Somebody once said to me, "In the process of change, don't wait until you are desperate for it. Make the change when you are still floating on feeling good about what you are doing. Let the process turn at that point, rather than waiting until you come down and hate it. Make the change when you are happy." I think that's a good idea. That's what happened with me. It seemed like a natural thing to make that change at that time. There's nothing wrong with losing a classroom teacher who through the process of growth says, "I'm going to do something else." What I hate is when a teacher says, "I'm burned out. I'm giving up."

I have a dream, or a hope, that public education can survive—and God, it needs some help if it's going to. It needs to change. It needs to be renewing for people who are in education. I think education needs a new look; I think it needs new leadership. I look at administrators everywhere and I say, "Come on, where's your pizzazz? Where's your verve?" I think we need a transfusion, and I think that can only come about through the kinds of personal changes we're talking about.

Maurice Ahrens
retired teacher, administrator, and college professor

The way I look at it, all the way through it's been not a career but an opportunity, an interesting experience. I started out going to a little liberal arts college. I got two years and then I didn't have enough money to go ahead, so I stopped and taught a year. I was principal of the high school, but I also taught in the elementary school. Callao, a little town, a little place in Missouri. In the county where I worked, except for the superintendent, I had the most education of any teacher in the county—with only two years of college. All you had to do to get a teaching certificate was take a very simple test. It was through the county; it wasn't a state affair. A lot of the teachers there had two years of high school and then taught in elementary. That was in 1922.

I got enough money to go back and finish my college degree. Then I took a job as superintendent of schools in Honeywell, a little rural community in Missouri. I stayed there for two years, and then I went home and visited my parents. I had lost thirty pounds, and my mother just got all excited. She took me to a doctor and they took an x-ray and said, "Well, you got tuberculosis. Go on out to Denver." So I went out to Denver, and came to find out this guy had made a mistake reading the x-ray.

In Denver I was sales manager of a brick and tile company. I worked at that for two years and I hated it. Made a lot of money, lots more money than I did in teaching. I went from one thousand, six hundred and sixty-five dollars a year as a superintendent to around six thousand dollars as a sales manager. But I hated it so that I took a teaching job in Lamar, Colorado for two thousand dollars a year, believe it or not. I loved teaching that much. If I did it all over again, that's all I'd do is teach. I love kids. I love little kids and I love big kids.

And another thing: I always taught from a practical standpoint. When I taught chemistry, I didn't follow the usual procedure. During the Depression, I had kids making their own cosmetics. They made their own hand lotions and their face creams and all that. I had them testing foods to see which was the best buy. I'd have them go out and buy six different brands of peas or six different brands of peaches. They would be responsible for opening the cans and checking the amount of sugar in there, the amount of liquid, the solid material, the quality of the food. They really had a deal.

Later on I got two other teachers in two other high schools interested in this, and we worked on it for awhile and then wrote a book called *Living Chemistry*, which was on the market from 1942 until 1972. It took us seven years to write it, working at night. Every night we met, we had a ping-pong table at each person's house and we'd play ping-pong for awhile and then we'd sit down and start to write. We had fun. Fact is, my experience in education has been pretty much fun all the way through. But serious fun.

Getting back to Lamar, I taught there three years and then the assistant superintendent came down there and saw what I was doing in chemistry and physics, and he said, "Look, we want you in Denver." So in 1931 I was hired in Denver. Times were bad then. There were only seventeen new teachers among two thousand teachers. I was really lucky. That's why I say this was an opportunity for me, all the way through. I taught in Denver in Manual High School. That was in a low economic level district, which I love to do. We had sixteen percent Mexican or Latin American; we had twelve percent Negro, blacks; we had eight percent Oriental; we had Slavs, Poles, and everything. But we also had some rich people coming there. We had a real cosmopolitan student body.

In 1937 they asked me to assume a supervisory role in the central office, a general supervisor for both elementary and secondary. I was really disappointed to leave the classroom, but I just felt like this was a challenge and maybe I could help some people. What I did, though, was I asked the superintendent: "Would you permit me to spend this first year actually going into elementary schools and teaching?" Which he did. So I taught in kindergarten, first grade, second grade, and on up through. I'd spend two to three weeks in each class. I spent six weeks in kindergarten, because I really like those little kids. That was a real education. I felt that if I was going to help teachers in the elementary schools, I had to renew my understanding of the curriculum and the kids and everything else. I had been at the high school level, and I didn't feel there was any problem there, but it had been quite a few years since I had dealt with elementary kids. I just felt like I needed more training. I'm delighted I did that. I would take over; I planned the curriculum and everything for that period. I thought that I could never really get the feeling of teaching those kids unless I actually took over. It wouldn't help me out just to be second-guessing the teacher. Of course, I had to talk with the teachers and ask them, "Would you permit me to do this?" I found some of them that didn't want me to do it, but I found some that did.

That was in '37. I worked with teachers for two years, and then in 1939 the American Council on Education was getting together a group of twenty people from all over the United States to work at Chicago University on human development. They chose me—don't ask me why, because I have no idea— and they paid my salary for a full year. There were several people who were leading the way in human development in those days. I was the only one in that group that didn't have a doctor's degree. We divided up into groups, and each one took some aspect of growth and went through all the research and then put it together. The sad part of it is, we put this all together and the leader of the group, who was supposed to take it and write a series of books, never did. He just didn't like to write. So except for the value it was to us, it has no value to education as a whole.

My background of working with children was enhanced when I got back by having all this information about human growth and development. It was a top-level educational experience for myself. I went back to Denver, and then they made me head of the Department of Curriculum Instruction, where I had about thirty or thirty-five supervisors under me. My responsibility was to work with these supervisors and get them to understand that you don't accomplish anything with a teacher when you try to dictate to them. My whole philosophy in education is that you work with people, you don't work at them or tell them what to do.

I moved from Denver in 1949. A superintendent came in there who didn't believe in what I was doing. He believed you ought to tell teachers what to do, how to do it, and when to do it. I don't believe in that. I said, "Heck, I'm not going to stay here." I had two offers when I wanted to leave Denver. One was to be superintendent of schools in Grosse Pointe, Michigan. That's where all the rich people live, the Fords and all those guys. I said, "There's nothing there at all for me." I was also invited to become an assistant superintendent in Battle Creek, Michigan, which I was wise to take.

One unfortunate thing was that from here on I've gotten

more away from children. When you go into administration, you don't have the close contact that you ought to have with children. I kept up some contact, because I couldn't stand to sit in my office. I'd go out and visit teachers. I only visited those that I didn't upset, but I soon found teachers that I could go in their classroom and participate with them and have fun. But I didn't have enough contact to develop relationships with particular children. That's the sad part of it. I sure did miss those relationships, you bet'cha. But I still felt that maybe I'm performing a service, trying to move a school system where they're browbeating teachers to where they're allowing them to participate. This is what I thought I was doing. I may not have done it, but I sure tried hard.

One thing I've always done in every school system, I form what I call a Committee on Instruction, where every school is represented. I meet with them and talk about curriculum development and give them a chance to make decisions about things that they think are important. I had that in Denver, I had it in Battle Creek, and I had it later on in Corpus Christi, Texas. They appreciate it. They like to have some say in what the curriculum is going to be. It improves their morale, no question about it. And that improves their teaching performance. I think there's a high correlation there.

I was in Battle Creek for just two years. They invited me (I've never applied for a job in my life) to come down to Corpus Christi, Texas, where they didn't have a curriculum department. They said, "If you come down here, we'll let you hire all your curriculum department members." I thought, "This is a great opportunity." Every place I had been before, the supervisors were already selected. I went down there and hired fifteen supervisors, people I knew about and knew the work they were doing.

The trouble there was the superintendent that hired me resigned to take a job as the head of a junior college. The guy that came in after him, he hurt me. He stabbed me in the back. He'd say it was all right to do this and all right to do that, then he'd turn right around and get you. I only stayed there three years.

Fortunately, the University of Florida invited me to come there for an interview, and then they hired me. I went there to teach, and I taught there one year, full-time. Then they said, "Now look, we've got to have a head of our Department of Elementary Education. We'd like to have you be head of Elementary." Which I did. I was five years doing that, then they asked me to be Assistant Dean. Which I did. But I got to teach a little bit all along the line, usually one course each semester. In addition to that, I also directed dissertations for graduate students; that is where I got the most personal contact.

Then I asked to be out and teach again, just because I wanted to. I wanted to have more contact with students, and they gave me three classes each semester instead of only one. Then the Dean said to me, "Look, I've got to have somebody the head of Curriculum Instruction." So I did that for three or four years. I did these administrative jobs only because of my great respect for the Dean. This fellow was a real fine person who operated a democratic college. I respected him, and therefore if he asked me to do something I would do it for him. I did continuously put in a request to go back into teaching, but he only let me do it that one year.

I'd like to have done more teaching, but I always kept at least one course and I did have those doctoral students. It was reasonably satisfactory. I never felt bogged down by my administrative duties, because when you involve people you have a different situation than when you have to sit at the top and make all the decisions. You don't feel worried to death that you have to make this decision or that decision. You make those decisions together. Democracy in education is more satisfying emotionally, especially if you're an administrator.

Well, I've been real fortunate. When I went out as head of the Department of Curriculum Instruction, that's when I had to retire because I had reached the age of seventy. I didn't retire at sixty-five because I was still having fun and enjoying it so much. I figured, "Why stop?"

But now that I'm retired, I'm having more fun then I ever had in my life. I'm still in good health. I'm eighty years old and I feel like I'm sixty. I'm working with senior citizens in R.S.V.P. What I do is I take, say, plumbing, and I develop these questionnaires for plumbers that say, "How much do you charge for your service call? Does that include any work? How much do you charge an hour? Do you have a discount for senior citizens?" I go to all the plumbers and get all that information from them and I put it on a chart. Then that goes out to three or four thousand senior citizens in Gainesville. I've done plumbers, I've done banks, I've done pharmacies, I've done electricians. Now I've got my questionnaire all fixed out for air conditioning and heating. Then another one I'm doing is for physicians. I'm really going to get knocked down on that one, but I'm going to try it.

I'm also a nut on growing plants. When I first retired, I had a place out on a lake, a couple of acres there, and I built myself two greenhouses. I grew plants, and then I'd sell them to retailers. I had eighteen citrus trees, great big high ones that I'd started there before I ever retired. I had almost every kind of fruit that you can imagine that will grow in a semi-tropical area. Then I had my heart attack there (thank goodness it was very mild), and I sold my lake place because it was too much. I couldn't give up growing plants, so now I have a greenhouse at my place in town. Twice a year I have a garage sale, and I sell my plants at about half price just to get rid of them. I give away as many as I can. Every one of my friends knows that they can come over and pick anything they want and take it home with them. It's the growing of them that gives me pleasure, and to spread them around.

My only involvement in education now is through these projects. I like to help people with problems that have to do with growing plants. I have all kinds of people that come and say, "What d'ya do with this? What d'ya do with that?" I try to help them. But as far as being in the college or anything like that, I'm not involved in it. I figure this: the rest of the time I have to live, if I can have a new interest, a new field to tackle, this will contribute to my well-being. I've always felt that I had to do different things that I was interested in. I don't know, I may do something else again. I don't know what it would be, but if something comes along that I feel very much interested in, why I'll do it.

Looking back on it, I don't think I could have stayed as vital and as interested if I had just stayed in one job all my life. That would have pushed back this feeling that I need new experiences, and that would not have been good. I don't mean to say that everybody is this way. I have friends who are teaching and that's all they want to do, but I'm not made that way. Even if I just taught, I'd want to go on and have different experiences, go to a different age level or a different subject or something.

Maybe that's why I went along and took these administrative jobs, even though I'd sometimes get frustrated from dealing with my superiors on a political level. I never had any frustrations with students. Oh, I had a ball with kids. That's a little bit of a puzzle to me, why I would choose to work with adults, since they were the ones that gave me the problems. The only way that I can explain that is when I looked at the job I was going into, in many cases it wasn't operating the way I thought it ought to operate. I thought maybe I could get in there and make a contribution. That's about the only reason I can think of. I would presume there was a little bit of ambition in there, but that was never the main factor at all. My wife and I used to talk this over, and I'd say to her: "Now look, if you think that what I'm trying to do is feather my nest, why I don't think we ought to do it." We talked it over pretty much before I made any kind of a move. I had to feel really sure that this was an opportunity and a chance to do something worthwhile. That sounds kind of like patting myself on the back, but that's the way I feel. I can't help that.

Commentary

William Nicholas and Bill Honig chose to leave the classroom to pursue hierarchical careers in education. Like most administrators, they have risen through the ranks: they put in their time in the classroom, but they did not want to stay there. Administrators are not always possessed with the personal warmth and patience required of regular teachers. They tend to be more interested in curriculum development, structure, or planning than emotional nurturance. They tend to be more involved with ideas or institutions than with children. Often, they think back on their classroom experience with fond memories, and perhaps they were good teachers for their period of service. But teaching was not enough; if it were, they would have remained in the classroom. For one reason or another, they wanted to climb.

Yet the notion of climbing seems a bit anachronistic in the field of education. An aura of service pervades the schools; if a teacher wants to seek fame or fortune, he might more appropriately go elsewhere with his worldly ambitions. Sometimes this happens, but often it does not. An ambitious teacher generally perceives education as his profession, and that is where he will choose to make his mark. From his position at the bottom of the ladder, he sees a host of challenging possibilities: counselor, supervisor, curriculum developer, program coordinator, vice-principal, principal, superintendent. The jobs are varied, but they all have one thing in common: none of them involves working with a room full of children. This one basic fact sets administrative jobs irretrievably apart from teaching jobs: they are totally different beasts. Separate as they are, they can hardly even be classified as part of the same profession.

In truth, the classroom teacher moving into administration is not just moving one step up on the old ladder; he is starting to climb a fresh one. He is playing in a brand new ballgame.

The rules are different; the rewards are different; the perils are different. The administrative game requires different talents and abilities, and it is suited to different tastes and personalities. It has a competitive aspect that is lacking from the tenured security of classroom teaching. It is a game of winning and losing, hiring and firing.

And there are many more losers than winners. There is simply not enough room in administration to accommodate all the classroom teachers who are restless for change. Hundreds of aspiring applicants toss their hats into the ring for a single job, yet all but one will be disappointed. And as in any competitive field, success is evasive, always one rung higher on the ladder. Not many people can make it to the very top. There are more disillusioned principals like William Nicholas than rising-star superintendents like Bill Honig. And no victory is permanently insured. Defeat is always just around the corner. On the lower echelons, head-hunting is common sport; on the higher echelons, jobs become increasingly subject to the whimsies of political fashion. A few years down the line, it is altogether possible that Bill Honig's ideas will once again fall out of vogue and he will be forced into retreat, relinquishing his prestigious position to the salesman for some new set of ideological beliefs.

Why, we might ask, does a teacher's quest for change so often lead to this competitive jungle? When a teacher gets restless, the easiest way out is to look for relief in the socially prescribed manner. Since administrators get higher pay and prestige than teachers, people tend to assume that their positions are objectively more desirable. So restless teachers wind up striving after those jobs, whether or not the higher positions are truly suited to their tastes and talents. Their choices seem circumscribed by a stratification that might have little bearing on their actual interests.

But is climbing really the only way to quench the thirst for change? Isn't it possible for teachers to pursue some other path to mobility, a path that won't necessarily force them to run on a hierarchical treadmill?

Carolyn Ruis and Maurice Ahrens did not try to climb the ladder just for the sake of climbing, but they still left the classroom in pursuit of change. Mobility has been the key to Maurice Ahrens's happiness and Carolyn Ruis's self-actualization. Their mobility, however, is a bit of an anomaly. They are both very talented, and they both have been fortunate in their opportunities. Maurice Ahrens is blessed with such personal charisma that he never filled out an application for any of the ten different jobs he has held. Most teachers, unfortunately, must carve out their careers with less ease and grace. Although it is tempting to hop around from one job to the next in an attempt to turn a basically static profession into a fluid one, an increasingly constrictive job market has forced teachers to cling tenaciously to their present jobs rather than venture forth into uncertain futures. In the context of modern education, Maurice Ahrens's career is the exception that proves the rule: his path is an enviable one, not likely to be duplicated by very many classroom teachers.

Maurice Ahrens has only one regret: the cost of his mobility was a separation from the youngsters. He was fortunate in maintaining some minimal contact; most administrators are denied any opportunity to teach. Administrative positions, because they involve no teaching, are sometimes called "noncombatant jobs"; the classroom, by contrast, has been labeled the "educational battlefield"—as if teaching were in fact a kind of war between the generations. It is the supreme irony in the field of education that status and pay seem to be measured by how little time the grown-ups are forced to spend with the children. Because of the inflexible dichotomy between teaching and administration, coupled with the lack of stratification within the field of teaching itself, a teacher who wants to advance in his profession must first abandon the basic hallmark of his trade: the classroom.

There is no inherent reason for the teaching profession to be this rigid. Other professions are apparently more fluid. Lawyers, for instance, can rise to a partnership in their firms, they can gain influence and prestige in the legal field, they can increase their starting salary five- or tenfold—and all this can be done within the normal context of their careers. They do not have to abandon their clients and the courtroom to achieve success. And success is only part of the story. Each new case a lawyer takes on involves new precedents, new research, new intellectual challenges. He does not have to teach the same old curriculum, year in and year out, to people of the exact same age. He does not have to go back to school or search through the papers for job openings in order to tackle new frontiers.

These are the kinds of fluidity which are lacking for teachers. But do they have to be lacking? Certainly, with a little imagination, we should be able to integrate professional change into the natural flow of the teaching experience. The evolution of a teacher's career should not have to lead directly out of the classroom.

Recently, two basic proposals have been presented to provide teachers with realistic avenues for advancement within a classroom setting: merit pay and a master teacher program. The merit pay idea promises to reward quality teachers with higher salaries, while the master teacher program promises to reward quality teachers not only with higher salaries but also with greater authority and prestige. On the surface, these proposals have compelling validity. Since nobody could possibly argue with the fundamental notion that "pay" should somehow be connected with "merit," the words themselves argue persuasively in behalf of the idea. Similarly, the words "master teacher" connote an image of something that people want to believe in: an exceptional, charismatic leader, maybe even a guru. Perhaps by simple appellation and legislative fiat such people can be made to exist.

Politicians seem to like these ideas because they are catchy reforms that the general public can easily understand. Influential leaders in private enterprise like these ideas because they are based on their own economic models. Nonteaching educators often like these ideas because they seem to validate that same ambition that has driven them out of the classroom. And yet, strangely, neither idea has received a great deal of support from the teaching community itself. Why are teachers so hesitant to embrace the very programs that promise to lift them out of their doldrums?

Both ideas hinge upon a fair and accurate evaluation of merit. But most practicing teachers seem to feel that the art of teaching is just a bit too elusive to permit such an objective evaluation. Then there is also the problem of rivalry and competition. Competition makes sense when the rules of the game are obvious, but why should teachers be made to compete with each other in a game where the rules can never be clearly defined? Realistically, overall morale is likely to suffer when we single out only a handful of teachers to be "meritorious" or "masters"—thereby implying that the rest are merely ordinary, not worthy of any special accolade.

The basic trouble with both these ideas stems from their linearity: they assume that teachers only want to move in a single, channeled direction—upwards. The ideas remain constricted within a hierarchical framework and are therefore incapable of addressing the full range of teachers' interests. They treat teachers as mere rats on a treadmill, not as multifaceted individuals with diverse needs and desires. They are, perforce, one-dimensional solutions to multidimensional problems.

Sadly, there is no single answer to the basic problem of how teachers can be kept alive and inspired in their work

as the years flow by. There are directions we can take, but our
troubles are not about to disappear by using a catchy political slogan or a one-dimensional solution. That would be
nice: find the words, rally behind them, and solve the problem once and for all. Unfortunately, neither the professional
needs of teachers nor the institutional realities of our work
are quite that simplistic.

Our only answer, insofar as it can be expressed in gen-
eralized terms, is an attitude, a dynamic approach to the
relationship between institutions and workers: teachers' jobs
should be flexibly structured to permit personal evolution and
professional development in the workplace. In practical terms,
this approach can be manifested in a myriad of forms appropriate to individualized circumstances. Let us take a look,
for example, at some real-life case histories of teachers who
seem troubled by the current state of their professional careers.

Rae Johnson (pp. 32–37) seems worn down by her job and
by her own high expectations, which are not always achieved.
The children are getting to her; she is tired of showing them
her tricks. She says, explicitly, that she would like more
support and feedback from parents and teachers. She needs
more contact with adults to keep her on the ball.
There are many forms this contact could take. She could
visit other teachers' classrooms, and they could visit hers.
She could take on some form of adult education project. She
could develop some of her classroom programs for export to
other teachers and other schools. She could lead workshops
in which she might share her expertise in specified areas;
she could attend workshops put on by her colleagues. None
of this is happening for her. Why not? Because she must
remain with her one group of children throughout the school
day; afterwards, she has no energy left to take on these extra
projects. What she needs is for these other opportunities to
be made accessible to her within the context of normal working hours. This raises some administrative problems, but the
problems are not insurmountable. It's a question of priorities.
If a teacher's professional rejuvenation is seen as a necessary
and worthwhile project, the required time and facilities can
be made available.

Frances Marinara (pp. 59–67) is not tired out by children;
it's the adults who wear her down. Yet precisely because she
wants to stay in the classroom, she remains stuck in a sub-
ordinate position where she suffers humiliation by her superiors. What she needs is a lift from her inferior status, but
not a lift that would remove her from the children. One

possibility would be to become a counselor. But counselors are not teachers, and she still loves to teach. What if she could become both a counselor and a teacher? That would certainly suit her tastes, and it would give institutional recognition for her special ability to communicate seriously and respectfully with children. She would be rewarded, not punished, for wanting to continue to work with the youngsters.

Helen McKenna (pp. 68–77) is admittedly ambitious, but she too still loves to teach. She remains dedicated to her goal of fostering scientific inquiry, yet after twenty years in the classroom she feels it is time to make her move. In fact, she has just been appointed vice-principal in charge of curriculum and instruction—but to take her new position she has been forced, somewhat reluctantly, to give up teaching totally. This is not absolutely necessary. There is no inherent reason why administrators should not be allowed to teach in some capacity. Particularly for administrators in the area of curriculum and instruction, maintaining one foot in the classroom could be a valuable asset.

For Juliet Sherwood (pp. 87–93) it is time to gear down. Approaching retirement, she is understandably losing the desire to put in sixty or seventy hours a week at a single job. But she still has the expertise, and she also has the energy to share it with others. She is presently casting about for the appropriate mechanisms: part-time work, teacher training, program development. Will the institutions be flexible enough to handle this type of worker, with special skills but also special demands? If so, they will help bring her career to a happy ending; if not, they will be depriving themselves—and the children—of her unique talents and her charismatic presence.

Sage Looney's career in education (pp. 38–43) has come to a standstill. She was, in a word, overwhelmed by her brief experience with teaching. Eight hundred students, thirteen hundred students—it was all a bit extreme. To work with such numbers effectively is too much to expect of anybody. The institutions used her up: in her place they will hire some other young, inspired teacher who might last, if she is lucky, for two or three years. Meanwhile, Sage Looney's talents are going unused. If they are ever to be used again, the schools will have to come up with a more humane job description to offer her. Otherwise, the educational services of this competent and now-experienced teacher will be lost forever.

Steve Adams (pp. 44–50) is clearly ready for a change of scenery. Of course he is always free to quit his job—and in fact he has just done so. But his decision required him to

abandon his tenured security. *For other teachers in similar circumstances, that security would hold too much appeal—and they would remain at their jobs longer than they should. There are several other ways in which Steve Adams's type of restlessness could be handled: there could be an extended leave of absence; there could be movement offered within the district; there could be a personnel trade, either temporary or permanent, with another district. There could even be a trade with some other organization that isn't a school. There is a strong movement these days to bring outside talent into education; such arrangements might be made reciprocal, enabling teachers to experience the "outside world" for a year or two without the fear that their careers in education have been terminated. Perhaps, their restlessness resolved, they would return to teaching with renewed energy, or perhaps they would find greener pastures elsewhere. In either case, the idea is to offer a counterbalance to the inertia caused by guaranteed job security. Teachers have become trapped by their own laws of tenure, fearful of giving up their automatic paychecks in order to face an uncertain job market. They often feel stuck, unhappy with their work and unhappy with themselves for not being able to quit. And the schools suffer too, for they are left with teachers who would rather be elsewhere. There are good reasons for tenure; it should not be abandoned—but teachers and administrators alike would do well to seek out innovative programs which facilitate the mobility that tenure seems to destroy.*

There is nothing particularly startling about any of these ways of dealing with teacher distress: increase job mobility, lighten the workload, allow for part-time teaching, involve the teachers in teacher training, allow administrators to teach and teachers to administrate, let teachers develop new curricula, let them share their expertise with each other, let them visit each other's classrooms and give each other feedback. It all sounds so rational, obvious, even trite. Unfortunately, such opportunities are rarely made available to any significant extent. The fact that these ideas are all so obvious—and yet so rarely practiced—is an indication of how little priority is given within education to the need for teacher rejuvenation. The notion of "teacher" remains abnormally constricted to exclude these opportunities which would help foster our collective renewal.

Of course it's not always that bad. There are some cases in which educational institutions have demonstrated more flexibility in behalf of teacher rejuvenation—and that flexibility has apparently paid off well. Witness, for example,

the stories of David Reynolds, Annie Waugh, and Carolyn Ruis, each of whom has gone through a career crisis and emerged on the other side with renewed energy.

David Reynolds's problems (pp. 51–58) were ostensibly personal. As he entered his midlife crisis, he decide to venture out on his own. What he discovered, much to his surprise, was that he really missed the social intercourse he had experienced in teaching. His school, familiar with his excellent teaching abilities, hired him back on a part-time basis. He took on some administrative duties—just enough to convince him that he would rather be a teacher than an administrator. The school stood behind him through his troubles, and it continued to stick with him as he attempted to overcome his alcoholism. This took some administrative flexibility, since his classes had to be covered for a month in the middle of the spring semester when he entered his treatment program. That month proved to be a profitable investment for Community High School, which now enjoys the services of an experienced, mature, yet very inspired teacher, with renewed dedication to his work.

Annie Waugh (pp. 78–86), after some unfortunate experiences with callous administrations, finally found a job in a district which treats its teachers respectfully. Crucial to her current success in the classroom is her chance to receive meaningful feedback from other adults: her administrator and her student teachers. Her involvement in teacher training helps to stimulate her own ideas, to keep her fresh. Under a sympathetic administration, she has managed to find ways to receive the necessary input for continual renewal on a daily basis.

Carolyn Ruis (pp. 115–119), needing a change after fifteen years, decided to work with adults instead of children. Fortunately, her district had a workshop program which enabled her to make the change she desired. She did not, at that point, want to follow the normal road into administration. She wanted to remain a teacher, although her students were now adults. In helping to rejuvenate other teachers, she naturally stimulated her own growth as well. Now, she is ready for another change: she wants to become a principal. But this time administration represents a conscious choice, not the path of least resistance. She feels she can be kept continuously renewed as long as she is permitted the types of professional exploration she has so far enjoyed.

Again, there is nothing particularly startling about these simple success stories. They are merely examples of teachers who have been treated by their employing institutions as

real people with personal needs and evolving professional interests. These problems were not solved by catchy political slogans which purport to provide a single answer for all teachers. Since the needs of each teacher are different, the natural paths toward rejuvenation must be individualized, tailor-made to their separate psyches. Somehow, each of these paths must be made accessible. However varied, each path must be encouraged and respected.

Structurally, the problem faced by the schools is how to provide a maximum number of opportunities for teachers to seek their work-related fulfillment—without always forcing them to abandon the classroom to find it. Presently, most of the challenging frontiers in education are open only to those teachers who are willing to give up teaching. Curriculum development, program planning, counseling, teacher supervision, district administration—the opportunities are there, but a teacher must first decide to stop being a teacher. A teacher's role is implicitly circumscribed by what he cannot pursue if he chooses to remain in the classroom.

This unnecessary limitation of possibilities stems from a structural inadequacy within the teaching profession. In this age of specialization, a whole new class structure has been inadvertently created within most professional fields, including education: on the one hand, there are the approved experts who have been skimmed off the top to deal with areas of increasingly narrow scope; on the other hand, there are the rest of the practicing professionals who are left behind to deal with the everyday problems—excluding those challenging fields which have developed their own specialists. In teaching, I question the merits of this increasing polarity. For the classroom teachers who are left behind, there can be a nagging sense of boredom, and perhaps failure, which saps their vitality. Yet even the teachers who advance into their various areas of specialization suffer from a polarization. They lose the connection which validates their work; they must practice their new art in a vacuum. Unless they remain plugged into specific teaching situations, their work becomes an abstraction. Good people though they may be, they slowly lose touch with the students and with the teaching experience. They lose their vested interest in the daily development of children; they lose their vested interest in the well-being of practicing teachers. They become a class apart.

What I am proposing here is to break down this polarity between generalists and specialists. I am suggesting that we find ways to broaden our choices, to change the rules of the

game so that teachers do not have to climb right out of the classroom in their pursuit of professional happiness. What we need is a wide variety of paths toward rejuvenation, which compliment rather than contradict classroom teaching. Collectively, these new opportunities can help to alleviate our boredom and overcome our fatigue. They can give us a new sense of definition and meaning.

The professional rejuvenation of our country's teachers constitutes an educational reform of major proportions. When teachers become stale, the children are bound to suffer—and so is society, which is counting on the schools (perhaps more than it should) to educate and socialize its youngsters. Conversely, when teachers become rejuvenated, the quality of their work is bound to improve, and the students, intuitive and perceptive, are bound to respond. When I speak on behalf of teacher rejuvenation, I am therefore speaking on behalf of education itself. This, I admit, is an assertion of self-importance. I am placing teachers at the hub of the educational experience. We mediate between childhood desires and adult expectations; we facilitate the transition from one generation to the next; we help form a bond between the past and the future. If, collectively, we teachers seem to be "losing it," we will be transmitting a dangerous message to the young ones: we will be telling them, inadvertently, that life is just ain't that great. Do we really want to foster such cynicism? Is that the image of the world we wish to project onto future generations?

I think not, and that is why I am now crying out for an improvement in teachers' collective morale. In order to improve our morale, I am suggesting a democratization of our workplace and an extension of our opportunities. These, of course, are self-serving positions. And yet, because of the unique nature of the teachers' role, these issues extend beyond our own self-interest. The psychic health of the teaching force is everybody's business. All of us together, teachers and nonteachers alike, have a vested interest in the viability of our educational system. The loss of teacher morale threatens to undermine that viability; teacher rejuvenation, on the other hand, promises to strengthen it.

Strangely, this results in a rather strong bargaining position for teachers. "Treat us right," we might say to the general public, "or we will not do right by your children." A bizarre power, indeed—almost blackmail. And yet this power is unavoidable: if we are not treated right, we will not be capable of doing right by the children, even if we have the best intentions. Our power is not malevolent; in fact, it is illusory.

As public servants, our job performance hinges on the financial, institutional, and psychological support we receive from our employers: the American people. It is the parents, citizens, and taxpayers who finally decide how good a job we will be permitted to do. Day-by-day, year-by-year, we await the public's decision.